Stone House Stories

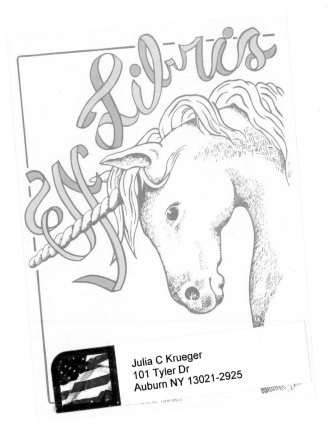

Stone House Stories

THE MEMOIR OF A
Free-Range Kid

KATHY LAWTON PURC

For information about this title contact the publisher:

Word Shed Press
Minden, Ontario, Canada
wordshedpress@gmail.com

The events and places in this memoir have been recreated from memory. Some conversations have been recreated and/or supplemented while remaining true to the relationships and events. The chronology of some events has been compressed.

Photo credits: Auburn, New York street scenes: Courtesy of Linda Butler; pages 57 & 131. Home Bureau Creed: Courtesy of New York State Federation of Home Bureaus, Inc.; page 52. Author photo: Danielle Meredith Photography; back cover. Cover photo and all other photos from the author's private collection.

ISBNs:
978-1-7771058-0-8 (print)
978-1-7771058-1-5 (eBook)

Printed in the United States of America

Cover and Interior design: 1106 Design

For Danny

Contents

Contents

The Leprechaun House

By Kathy Purc

There you stand, little house of stone,
The children grown, you seem alone.
Your walls have crumbled here and there,
And left your framework somewhat bare.

Your garden now has gone to weed.
Of color and beauty, have you no need?
Once elfin lilies fragranced your air,
Now daffodils and tulips no longer care.

What's become of you, will it happen to me?
Lost in time where no one can see,
Alone, forgotten, weathered and worn,
With a heart that is broken and ever forlorn.

I remember when I was a child at play,
In your garden with fairies who bid me to stay.
You took in our treasures of golden doubloons,
We'd captured from pirates in fearsome lagoons.

Treasures so many and treasures so deep,
Secrets, oh secrets, you promised to keep.
My childhood days are with you as well,
But it's time for the storyteller to tell

The world of the treasures and wonders you hold.
That storyteller may need to be bold,
To unlock your door and set them free,
Those stories about you and those about me.

They are stories of love and of laughter and tears.
Gathered like jewels over the years,
Many the mile I've carried them home.
Time's come at last for them to roam.

So, in ages to come, when we'll not be here,
My children's children may draw us near.
And know of our sorrows, our triumphs, and fears,
And know of our happiness told with our tears.

This bond now so strong between you and me,
Will give them their treasured legacy.
For search they will, some restless morn,
To know who loved them before they were born.

Walking the Edges

*P*repare, plant, hope, harvest. The farm cycle is hitched-up tight to the seasons. Round and round they go.

But, weather, now that's the moody one. An angry deluge or an obstinate drought can spell ruin. It's a risky business. Raising crops, tending a garden, or living a life.

Farmers take a long view to ride out the ups and downs. Children don't have a long view. Their lives are a rushing stream of now-moments. When recalled decades later, their memories are a jumble of paragraphs with no logical story line; a five-hundred-piece puzzle without its guiding image.

Some unsettling memories and nagging questions from my 1950s childhood urged me to return to that time and place for a closer look. As good luck would have it, my child-self was planted in the Finger

Lakes region of central New York State; a landscape of rich farmland, well-aged woodlands, and over four hundred miles of shoreline, not counting Lake Ontario's.

Our nearest neighbors back then, and the most aged, were Louis and Estella Mosher. To each other, and the neighborhood, they were Lou and Stell. Though tractors had been on the scene for many years, Lou held out against them. His two draft horses, Queenie and Duke, pulled the plow through Lou's sloping fields.

A deep lean-to, closed at both ends, stretched the full width of the south side of their time-worn house and shielded the kitchen door. The wide-open side of this practical add-on reached out toward any visitor walking up the laneway and waved them in; especially if they were a curious child. Rustic wood shelves, roughhewn benches, and cast-off cupboards staged a mesmerizing show. Retired kerosene lanterns kept close company with the weary stone crocks while the raw edge of a paint-flecked table steadied a rusted seat disembodied from a horse-drawn cultivator. Snugged up to the wax-dripped candle mold, a round wicker basket corralled loose pieces of dried-out leather harness. Guarding all of this with its toothy sneer was the lanky, two-person sawblade standing on end in the far back corner.

Once a child had dilly-dallied past half the distance of this eye-feast, the sweet spicy smell of a baking apple pie reached out and yanked the kid straight to the screen door. After a few small knocks, Stell's low, butter-soft voice would call out, "Well look who's here," as she opened the door. When the child stepped in, the spicy pie fragrance blended with the homey aroma of the wood-fired cook stove.

Neighborhood children were often treated to a piece of pie and the chance to "wow" over the faraway lands that popped out at them from Lou and Stell's ancient and mysterious stereotype viewer. But what stuck to their skin and drew them back again and again, was not the lure of this private museum. It was the mischievous gleam in Lou's eyes and his ready laugh. It was Stell's sweet, gap-toothed smile, lighting her full round face on which a flock of delicate freckles had landed. Gracious hosts, these two stopped whatever they were doing to wile away an hour with a child.

Stell sat in her rocking chair. Behind her, a window framed a wild outdoor scene of surrender. Shrewd weeds and tall grasses of opportunity staked their claim on the once-trampled barnyard. The child sat opposite Stell, on an armchair upholstered in needlepoint. Completing the cozy triangle, Lou sat captive in his unforgiving wooden chair with its two black iron wheels that were his only hope of moving. One of Lou's horses had kicked out, catching Lou in the lower spine. Long medical stockings sheathed his too-thin, too-still legs.

Lou and Stell's weathered house, the leaning fence posts, and the grayed-wood barn had been standing decades in advance of the arrival of electricity and telephone service. The structures were built in a bygone era; one in which farmers followed a custom they called "walking the edges."

I imagine Lou, in his younger days, striding with a brisk gait along the borders of his fields and pastures inspecting the stacked stone or split-log fencing for shifts and openings. Windstorms and rain squalls may have triggered a breach. Or, a persistent, single-minded cow might have butted its way in or out; such is the nature of cows and the dual personality of fences.

Lou and a neighboring farmer may have met by chance while inspecting their common fence line. A welcomed pause and a friendly chat would include the weather, their crops, and the market for their surplus harvest. A final, "How's the family?" and, "Yours?" before resuming their rounds.

Done with chores, church, and Sunday dinner, the restless farmer might use this ritual as an excuse to wander in fresh country air and solitude. Often, the walk turned into a living prayer asking for the patience and fortitude to farm, at least for another year.

Walking its edges paced-out the slice of countryside wherein farm families, like Lou and Stell's, had found their place of purpose and belonging. Home and a livelihood. Pity the poor city dwellers whose boundaries of longing are not as well defined.

A decade ago, I began writing stories from childhood memories. It amused me when some defiant stories shaped themselves, though I was the intended author. Impatient to be outed, they mumbled, "We know what we're doing, just get out of our way."

Peering into childhood's shadows takes courage. Walking its edges may take most of a lifetime. The poet Lucille Clifton spoke to the lingering child within all of us, when she wrote,

> a voice from the nondead past started talking,
> she closed her ears and it spelled out in her hand
> "you might as well answer the door, my child,
> the truth is furiously knocking."

("*the light that came to Lucille Clifton*"; from *Good Woman: Poems and a Memoir, 1969–1980*)

Bloom Where You're Planted

I could have fallen out of the sky on my fourth birthday and landed right side up on my new, shiny red tricycle because that's the first time I can remember a me. But my older sister, Polly, said that's not what happened. She claimed, the sky, having first gone black and thundery, hawked me up from the back of its throat and spit me out like a wad of snot. Polly called it the worst day in history—her sixth birthday.

By the time my fifth birthday, Polly's eleventh, rolled around, she wanted to go to court to change her birth date. Mom, as judge and jury, rendered a swift verdict. "Nonsense." Then she put an end to the whole fuss by drawing a red icing line down the middle of our frosted birthday cake. She labeled one side Polly and the other side Kathy.

That year our shared party was outside on the picnic table. Our guests were my friend Barbie, and her twin sisters Joan and Judy, who were Polly's friends. When they got to . . . dear, Ka-a-a-thy in the second round of singing "Happy Birthday," a keen-eyed robin swooped down, took aim at the O in Polly and Bull's-eye!

You'd think that bird would have got the blame, but, oh no, Polly said I ruined her birthday, not to mention her whole life! I couldn't fault Polly for not wanting to share her birthday, but why blame me? I didn't pick the day.

To be fair, on most days that were not our birthday, Polly was a tolerable older sister who took her time brushing the snarls out of my hair. She had a knack for making sense out of any tangled mess that came her way. Strand by strand she set the world right.

Long-legged, with light brown hair that fell naturally into ringlets, she appeared fragile and angelic. And while she could be quiet and mild-mannered, as could our mom, both turned fiery and opinionated at a moment's notice. Add to the mix that Polly was a daddy's girl, and you have a trigger-ready, mother-daughter duo locked in a clash that warred and waned, but never lost its grip.

Our brother Billy was the middleman; three years older than me, three years younger than Polly. And like a badminton net, he calmly divided the two sides while never taking his eye off the birdie. And when it hit the top of the net and teetered, he decided which way it fell. I didn't blame him for taking Polly's side. It was less hassle. Besides, for a big brother, he sometimes came close to being nice to me. Like when none of his friends were around to play, he considered me better than nothing. So what if he held his nose the whole time?

Billy and I often played a game Black Bart the Outlaw, in which Billy cast himself in the role of Sheriff. As his deputy, my part was to pretend not to know that each time the sheriff heard the name of his arch enemy, Black Bart, he would, for about three seconds, freeze as if caught between the jaws of a huge vice. Then, with wild-eyed contortions of face and flailing of limbs, he would bellow out threats and silly nonsense, and finally convulse into the throes of an apoplectic fit.

"So, Sheriff Billy, I hear there was a bank heist over in Twin Forks," I'd say in my exaggerated stage voice. "And they say the robber was some guy named (and this part I'd drag out as long as I could) Black Ba-a-a-a-a-a-r-t!"

Something about the sound of that final "t" set him off into his frenzy and I, having pulled the trigger, ended up wrestled to the ground, or shot off my horse, or tied to a tree, or locked up in jail. And only when I could stop laughing over his antics would I be untied, allowed back on my horse or sprung from the slammer. It never occurred to me or to Sheriff Billy to revise the script. I was typecast, like Wile E. Coyote, to make this same sorry mistake over and over and over again.

Billy was athletic, laid back, and wildly adventuresome. He grew those same long Lawton legs, straight, dark brown Lawton hair, and dark brown Lawton eyes. Polly and I agreed on one thing, he was Mom's favorite. Mom thought Billy could do no wrong. Huh!

Mom and Dad were the quintessential opposites who attracted. Mom had as much willpower as won't-power. If Dad said she was being stubborn, Mom said she was "determined, that's all."

Dad, being from a small Protestant family, was understated and reserved. Mom was from a large, boisterous Italian Roman Catholic family. At the time they first met, he lived in Auburn, New York's WASP-ish East End. She was ethnic West End. He was country/basic. She was city/style. He, a quiet loner. She, a chatty social butterfly. Dad was mechanical. Mom was creative. Dad, tall at 6 foot 1, Mom only about 5 foot 3. Dad was right-handed. Mom, a lefty.

Mom was a labeler, and the labels stuck. Once she made up her mind, she hardly budged. Mom critiqued people, places, and things through a spectrum she limited to four colors: black, white, right, and wrong.

Dad was damn sure there was a need for shades of gray, especially when he was being critiqued. His grittier spectrum of lenient colors included some troublemakers; notably, brewery-gold, bright-swear-word-blue, and orange-as-a-Protestant-from-Ulster.

Which of these two human opposites was the magnetic positive and which the negative depended on the topic and level of disparity. Mere disagreements were often resolved in short-order while Polly, Billy, and I looked on. However, if a ground skirmish broke out, the first shot between them was fired in private and the negotiated truce also signed in private. Their disputed issues on these occasions remained a mystery to us. Often, they clammed up and their reciprocal silence became their weapons of choice. In that case, Polly, Billy, and I were pressed into service as runners between the two camps.

"Kathy, tell your mother I'm going to the barber shop."

"Well, tell your dear, dear father, not to get lost!"

I dutifully delivered both messages word for word. If Dad grinned, I knew we would all survive. If he tightened his face, exhaled, and turned on his heel, I knew I'd be Monkey-In-the Middle for the prickly and bumpy long haul.

In the same way that two negatives make a positive, the opposite of two opposites is unity. When Mom and Dad were aligned, they were a formidable duo with shared values and robust standards. Together, by their everyday actions, they decreed:

1. Lawtons were always on time.

2. Lawtons were kind and respectful.

3. Lawtons were clean, neat, and well groomed.

4. Lawtons were honest and loyal.

5. Lawtons bought the best they could afford in cash, not on credit, then cared for it fiercely, hence it would last and last and last, ad infinitum.

6. Family was the highest priority.

7. If it was worth doing, Lawtons did it right.

8. The first time.

9. Lawtons were organized and dependable.

10. Lawtons worked hard.

11. Lawtons kept their word.

12. Lawtons had great hair.

That being said, and we being children, any lasting lessons in meeting the Lawton Standards were earned and learned the hard way.

All good stories start with a cast of characters (see above). Next, conflict must ensue (see above). Following that, a setting must be established.

Coincidentally, in 1946, Miss Destiny was searching for a place to relocate this Mary-Bill branch of the Lawton family. Miss Destiny was in one of her literal moods, some would call it lazy. She whisked us off her to-do list onto the one plot of land that had our name written all over it. Our family name, *Lawton,* came from the Olde English words "laugh ton" or "hlaw'tun" which could mean land by a lake or farm on top of a hill. Our smallish farm lay, not just by one lake, but parenthetically enclosed by the eleven Finger Lakes. And standing by in case it was needed, Lake Ontario hovered less than an hour to the north.

Our parcel of land was just east of where the Cayuga Nation, part of the Iroquois Six Nation Confederacy, once had their main longhouse community. Both lie in Cayuga County, Town of Scipio (*Sip-ee-oh,* the "c" is silent). The town was named for the Roman general Scipio Africanus by an early New York State official, who in a fit of classical name-dropping left a mass of Central New York towns with enlightened names: *Manlius, Camillus, Ovid, Ithaca, Dundee, Hector, Marcellus, Camillus, Brutus, Mentz, et cetera.* The town of *Hannibal,* the same name of *Scipio's* archenemy whom he defeated at Carthage, lay just a few miles to the north.

The county seat and largest nearby city was Auburn, situated about nine miles north of Scipio. Auburn is best known for its imposing maximum-security prison; the home of William Seward, President Lincoln's Secretary of State who negotiated the purchase of Alaska from Russia; and the home and final resting place of Harriet Tubman, conductor of slaves on their journey to freedom by way of the Underground Railroad. Auburn's 1950 population was 36,722.

By contrast, the town of Scipio had 1,202 human residents. However, the Scipio Holsteins and Guernseys far outnumbered their keepers. Mounting a successful rebellion was thinkable. But, alas, no insurgent leader surfaced from the herds. Each critter's face wore one and only one expression identical to all its pasture-mates: a resting face.

A dairy cow's idea of a bovine coup was to saunter through a broken-down fence only to stand stock still in the middle of the dirt road. Puzzled by freedom they pondered their bounteous pasture grass, now out of reach. Good at breaking out, they never mastered breaking back in. The next moo-v-e was the farmer's.

An aerial view of our modest thirteen-acre property reveals it is shaped like a piece of apple pie. The narrow end points northeast and meets the intersection of Mosher Road and Cork Street at the bottom of "our" hill. The valley over which we looked to the east may have been scoured out by glaciers, as earth science suggests. Or, someone may have opened the oven door too soon and the land just dropped. But either way, we lived on the edge.

This farm on top of a hill, on land by a lake, was meant to be ours. If our name had been anything but Lawton, who knows where we would have landed or who else might be telling these stories.

Homespun

*M*y four-year-old life had its limits. Indoors, I had the run of the house albeit a small compact abode that made running a moot point. Built around 1865, the house had no use for hallways, interior doors, or closets; the things kids count on to run through, slam shut, or hide in. Nope. Economy reigned.

The largest room, the living room, was about 12 ft. by 12 ft. Jammed up next to it were the small kitchen and a den-like room. Upstairs and downstairs were connected by a narrow stairwell with a steep pitch and abnormally narrow treads; the house's one concession to kids. While unsuitable for adult-sized feet, the stairs were built so our kid-sized bottoms skimmed the edge of the treads, bouncing downward nonstop and lickety-split.

At no time did the house consider inhabitants to need more than two bedrooms. On this it stood firm. The large bedroom at the front, over the living room, was Mom and Dad's. Polly and I crowded into the much smaller one at the back corner of the house. Polly's bed was not a double, but a single-and-a-half size. My single bed was next to the window that looked out over Cork Street and the parallel running swamp. Warm nights and an open window welcomed the wild sounds from the swamp into our room. Spring peepers sang us to sleep. Wild geese woke us with a honking morning fly-by. And for two weeks of one summer an itinerant bobcat scared the bejesus out of us with its eerie nighttime wail.

Polly and I each had a small dresser, shelves above our beds and one desk meant to be shared. There was just enough floor space left to allow Polly to reach her half, which, like her bed, was a bigger half than mine. Billy's single bed and dresser took up most of the space on the upstairs landing with enough left over for a clothes rod on wheels. The house's unwavering conviction was close-knit rooms make close-knit families.

A thin wall with its doorless opening separated Billy's bed from mine and Polly's. Lying in our beds, Polly started a ghost story. Billy's voice, through the open doorway, added gory details. While Polly's wild man, with a hook for his hand, advanced toward his victim, Billy slithered from his bed and onto the floor. Like a lizard he crept undetected to the side of my bed. When Polly's wild man lunged for his victim, Billy jumped up beside me and roared. I screamed, then cried. As I got a little older, the same scenario made us all silly. Either way, it drew a parent's voice up the stairway, "simmer down up there."

Outdoors was a different matter. I was free to roam the large lawn as long as I did not cross certain boundaries. Mature trees, the pillars of my community, had taken strategic positions to remind me of those borders. I got to know each of these guardians on an individual basis as Dad rotated my rope swing among them from year to year.

Horse Chestnut with its grooved bark was the easiest to climb. One of its massive limbs curved low enough for me to curl up into its lowest crook. It felt like I was sitting in someone's lap. I often imagined that someone was the tall, dark, mysterious grandfather I had never known—long dead before I was born. I could tell from Dad's faraway look and soft voice when he talked of Grandpa Lawton that he loved and missed his dad. That was good enough for me. I would love and miss Grandpa Lawton too. This stalwart tree-friend guarded the eastern border of the lawn and reminded me to "stay outta the long grass, kid, you could get lost in there."

On the other hand, Maple had a smooth, slim trunk and wore a perfectly balanced coiffure that, by autumn, turned from pliable summer green to pure papery gold. Refined and reverent, she "lifted her leafy arms to pray" and stood watch to the north where the driveway met the road. Her gentle presence reminded me that "the road is no place for you, dear child; stay in the lawn, now, you hear?"

The only tree that gave us edible nuts was Hickory. Little treasures to break open between two rocks for a quick pick-me-up snack on a busy play day. While I never matched a gender to Hickory, it was friendly, steadfast, and generous. Hickory guarded the western frontier and kept me out of the vegetable garden and the cornfield beyond.

Black Walnut, rooted in the center of the lawn, had the easiest job. He stood cool, tall, and dignified like an aristocrat. His noble presence had no specific message, but he was always there for me, and we shared a secret. More on that later.

The south side had no tree, but Mom's flower gardens stretched across that part of the lawn. The tall, blue delphiniums had white eyes with black dots facing in all directions and lined up all the way down their tall stems. No matter which way I moved those hundreds of eyes watched me. They were Mom's garden favorites for which she had earned an envied reputation among neighbors and relatives. To me they were spooky. I knew they were somehow in cahoots with Mom. Whenever I accidentally went off course or out of bounds, Mom materialized from thin air just in time to set me straight.

These watchful flowers and looming trees were powerful reminders that my goodness and safety ran out at the grassy edge of the mowed lawn. Intent on being good and staying safe, I had no reason to venture near the dangers that lurked in the tall grass, the cornfield, and the dirt road. At least, not yet.

No Rose Without
a Thorn

On a sticky-hot August day during my fourth summer, Mom walked into the kitchen carrying four empty Easter baskets. Polly, Billy, our city cousin Carmen, and I were sitting at the table just finishing lunch. Reading the confusion on our faces, Mom explained she wanted to make a blackberry pie. We were to take the Easter baskets down the hill behind our house to the blackberry patch, fill them up and bring them back.

No-nonsense Polly led the way down the road intent on getting the job done, done right, done quickly. Billy and Carmen, the buddies, followed behind her, kicking up gravel trying to hit the back of Polly's legs. I followed them at the end like a caboose. I had become enchanted with the iridescent blue line on my Easter basket. I was focused on where it went and how it got up and over and down and around the pink and green lines that were both squarely in its way. I guess I was lagging.

We came to attention when Polly stopped, turned around, and snapped, "Billy and Carmen, cut it out! And you, Baby, if you can't keep up, I'm leaving you here for the wolves to eat."

Wolves? I ran to catch up. I didn't know wolves lived here. I thought they were just in my storybooks. But worse than the fear, was the sting I felt when Polly had hissed the word, Baby. Did she forget I'm four?

We reached the berry patch just off the edge of the road.

"Holy cow! There's a ton of 'em," shouted Billy, as if there was a comic book balloon hanging over his head with an arrow pointing to his mouth. Bam-Smack-Pow nicely summed up his basic demeanor back then (and even now, come to think of it). We started picking berries side-by-side but moved apart as one of us after the other shouted out our finds.

"Wow, I just found the mother lode."

After half an hour, Polly called us all together out on the road to judge the volume of our pickings.

"Enough," she pronounced, and up the hill for home we went. I felt proud to belong to this team that had accomplished its mission. And for the moment it erased the sting of the label Baby.

When we reached the kitchen, Mom held out a large stainless-steel pan. In our usual order, Polly was first to empty her basket into the pan followed by Billy, then Carmen. Polly laughed out loud when I added the entire contents of my basket, amounting to a scant hand-ful, a baby's handful.

"That's pathetic," she said.

"Yeh, Baby, that stinks," filled Billy's comic book balloon, except the smooth edges had grown sharp spikes.

Mom measured the berries and said that one more basketful of berries would be enough fruit for two pies and asked us to go back to the berry patch.

"Fine," said Polly. "But we're not taking Baby this time."

Mom surveyed me head-to-toe no doubt noting stained lips, scratched legs, and sleepy eyes. She declared it my nap time.

"Nooooooooo," I howled. "I wanna go."

"Not this time," said Mom.

Polly clapped her hands and hopped up and down.

Billy said, "Bye, bye, Baby."

Nice teammates they turned out to be!

When I looked at Carmen, he tipped his head a little to the side and his dark brown, puppy-sad eyes and apologetic smile told me that he wasn't in a position to change this course of events. His perceived kindness, however, was forever written on my rejected little heart.

Mom let me lie down on the living room sofa for my nap. From there I could see her standing at the kitchen counter making the pie crust. I pictured the huge mound of blackberries now washed and cooling in the refrigerator. My mouth watered, my legs twitched, and I slid off the sofa and into something new for me. Stealth mode. I tiptoed on socked feet into the kitchen, behind Mom's back, and slowly and quietly pulled the refrigerator door handle down to unlatch it. There at nose-height was the treasure. Not yet schooled in moderation, I lifted the whole pan with both hands off the shelf and set it noiselessly on the floor. Closing the fridge's door made just a little noise, but because Mom was humming and rolling out the dough, she never heard it. I tiptoed back to the living room with my treasure. Something told me not to sit on the couch, but behind it on the floor.

With the pan resting on my folded legs, I started shoveling them in. Gobs and globs of berries. Purple juice ran down my chin, onto my clothes and stuck my fingers together as the mound of berries lost most of its bulk. Then I started yawning and before I knew it, I was sound asleep.

When I woke up, I heard the ruckus as Polly, Billy, and Carmen poured into the kitchen from outside. The screen door whacked shut.

"Good job! How about some Kool Aid?" Mom asked.

"Yes," they yelled in unison.

I heard the refrigerator door open and then Mom said, "Well, where on earth are the berries?"

From here the rest of the story has had as many variations as it has had story tellers. I was never the one to tell it since it was always told in front of company to entertain them with my shame. But here is the true and accurate account of what amounted to my sweet revenge.

Polly said, "Where's Kathy?"

And Mom said, "I don't know. I checked on her once, couldn't find her, then went back to rolling my dough."

Polly said, "Well, if the berries are missing and that brat's missing, too, it only goes to prove, that one plus one is two. Let's find that brat of a sister. She couldn't be that far. I'll pinch her so hard she'll tell us where those blackberries are!"

Slowly, Billy and Polly pulled the sofa away from the wall. What they saw when they found me amazed them and left them quite appalled. Purple was I, from head to toe—my clothes—my skin—my hair. Oh! And the pan where the berries had once been held was, ahem, quite empty and bare.

"Kathleen Ann!" Mom's voice was stern, "What will I do with you?" But I could tell she was trying not to smile as she noticed my berry hue.

Polly and Billy stomped away. They were really, really mad. But as for me I could honestly say I felt sweetly, sweetly glad! My stomach, then, went flip and flop. The berries did not miss a beat. I felt them going the very wrong way on what once was a one-way street.

"We could have had two pies, you brat," said Polly that night at the table. "Instead, we have one. I'll get even with you the very first time I am able."

"Me too," said Billy. "I'll make it very scary if you ever, ever steal again; even one little tiny berry."

"Now, now!" said Mom, "She's only just four and she's learned her lesson well."

I thought to myself, "How right you are, Mom! I can make paybacks HELL!"

Of course, I didn't think or say those exact words, then. But I wished I had. From that time forward, subtle subterfuge was about as wild as I got and then only when boxed into a corner.

My infantile brain soaked up the whole blackberry experience knowing something unseen, magical, and working on my behalf had sprouted. It was the concept of personal power. A little bit more me in me. It was not enough to prime a pump, but that one tiny droplet was enough to quench my parched little soul. For the time being.

A Pig in a Poke

Despite the occasional prick of a needle, or a gag from a tongue depressor, visits to Dr. Eisenberg's South Street office in Auburn were miniadventures. An arched, canvas awning, striped like a circus tent, stretched from the street-front wall of the house and sloped down over the concrete steps that descended to his basement office. Down we went. My darting imagination fled the circus and flung us toward a secret cave. But as Mom and I entered, the bell above the door tinkled. No secrets here.

Dr. Eisenberg's waiting room was as cheerful as the awning. Toys stood ready to amuse pouty kids and those bored of coloring at the kid-sized table. My treasured spot was beneath the window next to the shelves overflowing with kids' books. A pity, our wait was never long enough for me to read through the tall stack I'd picked.

"H-m-m-m-m," was the official diagnosis for my fire-red tonsils. Mom listened as Dr. Eisenberg made his soft-spoken case for my tonsillectomy. With his New York City accent and his rimless glasses, he oozed expertise and confidence. Of slight build and impeccable grooming, the good doctor convinced Mom I was due for this medical rite of passage for four- and five-year-olds. Me, he bribed with the promise of unlimited ice cream after surgery. Why, yes, Dr. Eisenberg, sign me up!

History's first recorded tonsillectomy occurred in the first century BC performed by the Roman doctor Cornelius Celsus. He used nothing but his own fingers to remove the tonsils. The first century BC was devoid of anesthetic. And horror of horrors, there was no ice cream.

By 1950, this surgery became fashionable, which would have appealed to Mom. Sharp surgical blades became fashionable too. That would have appealed to Dr. Eisenberg. Thought to prevent recurring respiratory infections in children, tonsillectomies relieved 61% of kids of their tonsils between 1950 and 1970. Then, this surgery fell out of fashion, sorry, Mom, when a search failed to turn up scientific studies proving its efficacy.

I remember only three crystal-clear things about having my tonsils out. One, was my yearning for the gobs of ice cream afterward. Two, the cold, wet, brown square of scratchy wool cloth placed over my face. Three, the two-second whiff of pungent ether, then it was lights out.

Mom and Dad often recounted their story of my tonsillectomy as though by retelling it, they, too, could shake it off. I felt removed from their version as if I were watching a television show about me but starring some other kid.

They said that during my post-op period in the hospital, I was isolated in a glass-enclosed room with other small children for two or three days. My parents could look in, but they were locked out.

Mom narrated the part about watching my hysterics in the iron hospital crib. I rocked and banged my head against the bars by which I had been imprisoned. I was four, used to my single bed at home. Cribs were for babies.

Dad told the second part about how they fretted at not being allowed to hold me, calm me down, or at least let me know they were there. Nurses told them I'd been restrained in a crib at night to prevent me from injuring myself.

It was the first time I'd been separated from my parents for more than a few hours. At four, my nascent concept of time passing may have interpreted each minute without them, as forever. Take the cold sterile environment, add a dozen other anguished kids, their caterwauling bouncing off glass walls, and it's the recipe for my worst nightmare.

My anesthetized child brain couldn't name or even remember the feeling of abandonment. I suspect, that through what neuroscience calls *embodiment*, I may have internalized both my agony and my parents' distress from their storytelling.

Abandonment, intentional or not, hurts physically. It hurts all over. It hurts at the cellular level. It hurts when you're growing and when you're grown.

Loss of a beloved pet was abandonment. Loss of a love interest, whatever the reason, was abandonment. A disloyal friend betraying a confidence; all of these bring that same pain.

Time and self-fortitude are the only healers. An abundance of time.

In a perfect world the quick fix for the pain of mental and emotional pain would be ice cream. However, I've yet to find a flavor that delivers 100%. Though, Lord knows, I keep trying.

Sorting the Wheat
from the Chaff

Just before my fifth birthday, Polly's eleventh, she spun yet another story of how I came to be a Lawton. Her numerous story versions confused me. I didn't know whether I'd fallen out of the sky, slithered out from under a rock, or as in this newest variation, been found living with wolves by Indians. This latest tale claimed that I was raised in their teepee village until I was three and then the Indians left me on the Lawton doorstep—because I "smelled so bad."

None of her stories flattered me. I began to wonder why there were countless stories but only one of me. Even at that tender age, I sensed that truth was a place. And that place, was Mom.

Mom explained to me that Polly and Billy had been born in a hospital, not delivered by a big, white, sparkly bird the way Polly had told it. Mom didn't explain what born meant nor did I think to ask. But she did say that since I would be starting kindergarten in the fall, I should know the truth.

Before Billy and I joined the family, Mom told me, she, Dad, and Polly moved from Auburn to Buffalo when Dad took a job at the Bell Aircraft plant when the U. S. joined World War Two. Millard Fillmore Hospital in Buffalo was where Billy was born, then me. Because of the war, both doctors and anesthetics were scarce, even in maternity wards. With nothing for pain, Mom had been hoping for a quick delivery and things were going just that way for her and me. But the delivery nurse declared that Mom and I had to wait until the overworked and stretched-thin doctor arrived. And to make sure we obeyed, the nurse threw her whole body across my mother's belly to prevent me from being born. That not only increased the pain for Mom, but it, as Billy would later like to say, and say often, was the probable cause of my permanent brain damage.

The doctor arrived after a half-hour wait, removed the nurse, and let me be born to take my first breath. There's no certainty in tracing my occasional claustrophobia back to my birth story, but I can't tell it or write about it without stopping a few times to gulp air.

Before I even set foot into Mrs. Adams's kindergarten at Sherwood Central School, Polly taught me two life-changing lessons.

One, big sisters lie.

Two, if something doesn't feel right, it pays to ask questions.

Breaking New Ground

*K*indergarten is:

- ☆ The taste of vanilla ice cream from a waxed Dixie Cup. The slight melt around the sides makes the firm rounded center float. Cold. Vanilla. The flat taste of the wooden spoon, rough on my tongue.

- ☆ The smell of canvas from my folding cot for nap time. The smell of home on my colorful, Indian-design blanket I keep in my cubby.

- ☆ The freckles on Mrs. Adams's face and arms. Her curly, curly reddish hair.

✿ The sound of the big wall clock ticking away our nap time; or ticking me off, to sleep.

✿ The silky, cool blanket binding I rub back and forth between Pointer and Tall Man. Tick, tock, tick. . . .

✿ The swoosh of finger paint on the heel of my hand. Squiggling blue into a big swoosh. I think I'll swoosh in bright yellow. Twist a bow tie pasta back and forth in orange. A piece of rigatoni makes black tire tracks.

✿ Bumping into Katie because I'm daydreaming when our line comes to a stop.

✿ The cold iron bar I try to fold my hands around; I pull back and push forward; then it pulls me back and forth, as thirty of us make the wooden merry-go-round go as fast as we can. I am seventh from the right in the previous photo.

Riding the school bus every day was a portal to the wider world. I could see and make sense of where my family and I fit into the larger scheme of our immediate neighborhood. Sprawling dairy farms were interspersed with small plots of land like ours and those of the older couples, who had sold or rented their fields to the neighboring farmers. An abundance of hedgerows, woodlands, and swampland in and around farmers' fields delineated one snug, self-contained farm from another.

This rural pattern was persistent except where a few small hamlets got a foothold. Five miles to the south of Mosher Road on Route 34B, prolific farmland donned gracious blinders as Scipioville claimed the four corners made by Center & Levana roads. Its two dozen homes, small church, old country store, and a mechanic's garage huddled together to defy time.

Two miles further south, Sherwood, was a similar size, but included our school, and a museum that boasted a set of George Washington's wooden dentures. Six miles from our house to the southeast, the hamlet of Scipio Center had a solid character and unarguable reasons for taking up valuable crop land; a post office, town government office, mechanic's garage, two churches, and a big general store.

My world of people got bigger too. At school, twenty-seven classmates were twenty-seven new playmates. We were all in this together. We were equals. It was a fresh start. These new kids, unlike my siblings, had no built-in distaste for me. Teachers became more adults I wanted to please.

Sherwood Central School housed kindergarten, six elementary classes, two junior high grades, and four years of high school all in the same building. Polly, Billy, and I progressed through the same classrooms and were taught by many of the same teachers.

We marched to the beat of the pervasive alphabetical order of the 1950s. Lacey, Lawton, Minde. We said "here" to roll call in that order. We lined up that way to snake our way to the cafeteria for lunch. Our desks shared the space reserved for Ls and Ms. Katie Lacey and Sue Minde. We three became friends, while classmates in other letter groups grumbled and craved to mix things up. Many of my kindergarten classmates, including Katie and Sue, were partners in crime right on through to our high school graduating class of thirty.

Riding the school bus had other benefits. It introduced me to new playmates right in my own neighborhood and a means of transportation to each other's houses.

Our school bus stopped, as usual, at our driveway one Friday afternoon. Danny Desmond, the tough but affable gray-haired driver swung open the door. Sherwood bus #17 disgorged Polly and Billy. Spit them out like watermelon seeds or cherry pits. Ptewy!

But not me. I stayed seated with my pj's, toothbrush, and play clothes at my side. Twenty minutes later, the clouds parted, the sun shown, birds sang, bells rang, banners flew, as I alighted the bus with Barbie Van Liew at her family's home on Walters Road.

The next morning, Saturday, the aroma of bacon wafted up the stairs and slid under the door to Barbie's bedroom. It woke us after a later than usual night of giggling and planning our adventures for the next day. We bounced down the wide staircase and through the long hallway to the breakfast room. A whole room just for breakfast and a big dining room for other meals! I think the Van Liew house was big enough to hold at least three Lawton houses.

Barbie and I sat down at the table next to each other just as Myron, Barbie's dad, come in from the barn. He washed at the sink, came to the table, and said, "Well, the ladies are taken care of, let's eat." He was referring to his herd of dairy cows, their morning's milking and his chores completed.

Loretta, Barbie's mom, brought the potatoes, eggs, and bacon to the table to add to the orange juice and glass of milk at each of our plates. Gary, Barbie's brother, was a year older than me and was Billy's buddy. He sat across from me with his typical mischievous look popping up between bites. Further down the table were twins, Joan and Judy, Polly's friends. It figures she'd get more than her fair share.

I don't know exactly how the Lawton family met the Van Liew family, but we couldn't have been luckier. Loretta and Myron became card-playing, dinner-sharing, lifelong friends for Mom and Dad. Myron was a big, handsome, jovial fellow whose job it was to look after the "ladies" and to grow cash crops on their large farm. Loretta was pretty, petite, bouncy, and made the best chocolate cake with thick chocolate frosting.

Though Gary's farm work increased with his age, he and Billy still found time to explore and hunt. They were Little League teammates, Billy pitching, Gary catching. Both families gathered often at the Lawton picnic table to slice open a watermelon, celebrating a just-ended, nail-biting nine innings.

Joan and Judy were in the same class as Polly and shared the same friends. The twin sisters were usually sweet and kind to Barbie and me. They gave me the idea of the sort of sister I would have chosen if I'd had the chance.

Barbie was a year younger than me and a year behind me in school. But not much else separated us. We sat together on the bus, played dolls, played school, and played and played and played. An exciting afternoon for us was riding in the high-walled farm wagon hitched to the corn picker that was pulled by the tractor that was driven by her dad.

The tough, pointed ears of dried corn winged out of the corn-picker's tall chute, through the air, and into the wagon. Trying to dodge the unending flow of missiles with their unpredictable paths kept us in constant motion. The wagon had no shock absorbers or springs. As it navigated the ruts and valleys of the remaining rows of cornstalks, we were thrown this way and that with no hope of staying on our feet. The shaking we took didn't stop until a half-hour after getting our feet back on solid ground. Though it was a grueling, bruising way to have fun, it was one of my favorites.

In winter, when Gary's farm chores lessened, he'd hitch up his three sisters on their sleds to a tractor by way of two long ropes. Down Cork Street and up our hill they'd fly. With some careful rearranging of his trailing sisters, the train would get turned 360 degrees toward downhill. Polly, Billy, and I tied on our sleds/saucers to the ropes. Gary put it in gear and opened the gas and our chaotic procession flew down our hill and around the neighborhood. It was not a neat nor painless procession. One or more of us was thrown off and had to run to catch up; hoping Gary would slow down to let us. He was creative with his speed and quick change of direction. Two or more of us could get tangled up and flipped over and off into the snowbank. Despite the lack of helmets or any other safeguards that didn't exist at the time, we all survived, mostly undamaged.

Hitting the Nail on the Head

Our neighborhood had a good balance of young families with the older folks, the working farmland with the fallow, and the vintage homes with the more modern.

When we Lawtons moved into our house back in 1946, it was over eighty years old then. There was no indoor plumbing. A wooden two-seater outhouse complete with a crescent moon cut-out at its peak stood in the back yard. A stone cistern to collect and store rainwater loomed in the dank, dirt-floor cellar. The main convenience that existed was the hand pump at the kitchen sink. Outside, another larger hand pump stood over the outside well to draw drinking water.

My weekly bath water was hand-pumped at the kitchen sink into a pail, heated on the stove, then poured into a round galvanized steel tub that was stored in the cellar when not in use.

The floors were covered in linoleum, circa 1920s, I think. The living room floor sported a dark maroon background with a large, beige floral design.

The house may have been content in its antiquated ways, but my parents coaxed it into the midtwentieth century.

The cistern was decommissioned, and the well water plumbed into the house. The cellar, once its floor became cement, cried out that, henceforth, it should be referred to as a basement. A central furnace in the basement with duct work replaced the oil stove in the living room. Dad built a one-story addition onto the house that doubled the size of the kitchen, included a three-piece indoor bathroom, and an entry room to shield the front door that opened directly into the living room. Once the addition was complete, new tile covered the downstairs floors. In the living room, a neutral carpet updated the vibe and Mom sewed lined, pleated floral drapes for the windows.

Dad completed 99% of the renovation on his own. By himself. On weekends. Where he acquired the knowledge is a mystery to me. There was no one hired to dig the foundation for the addition. Dad did that himself with his pick and hand shovel. He also built the cement block frame and poured concrete for the foundation. He was the architect, builder, and sole tradesman for all of this as far as I know. All did not go without mishap or injury, however.

During the renovation, Dad's tools were prominent, and we became used to their presence. In fact, at least one legend was born. His one and only hammer, with no notice, went on sick leave when its steel head flew off its wooden handle. Dad fixed it with an irony that sent Mom into one of her trademark fits of tearful laughter. He expanded the narrow end of the wooden handle to once more fit snugly into the head's eye. He did this by driving into it two large nails. But with what? Had he simply commanded, "Hammer, heal thyself"?

Dad was frustrated if something wasn't going the way he planned. If the resurrected hammer was part of the fix, there was more to his pounding tempo than persuading a single nail to yield. Fear, uncertainty, a layoff from his job, the loss of a loved one, those times Mom would set her jaw and not give in. With his percussive therapy, Dad transformed our circa 1865 house to a more modern version. Mom contends the number of Dad's swear words that went into the addition outnumbered the nails two to one.

I liked to watch Dad building, especially if things were going well. I became his tool handler on those occasions. No matter how hot the day, the upper and lower flat steel planes of his black cast iron level were always smooth and cool to my touch. My index finger liked to trace the intricate curlicue design of its fretwork. Who had poured their creative soul into making this humble tool artful? I didn't know then, but the level was most likely a Davis ornate model made in the mid-1800s. I like to think it was passed down to Dad from his father who got it from his father. This level, like my dad, had a graceful authority and a quiet wisdom whenever something in life shifted out of balance.

Billy and I were told not to play in the ongoing foundation work, especially when Dad was away at work. But a plank was left spanning a four-foot gap between the old foundation and the new. It was too perfect for two pirates to pass up. Captain Peg Leg (offstage) ordered us both to walk the plank. Despite our made-up drama of hurricane force winds and a frenzy of sharks below us, I made it across safely. First Mate Billy made the mistake of overacting his response to the ship's wild listing. The board flipped and Billy plunged down to

Davy Jones's Locker. His head hit a sharp rock jutting from the old foundation. Blood ensued.

Billy lost a patch of hair. Orange iodine stung his scalp in advance of the four stitches to close the wound. Cap'n Peg Leg required no further retribution and sailed on. No such luck when Dad arrived home. We both caught verbal hell and some extra chores to make up for our transgressions. Right there and then, we turned in our eyepatches and quit the pirate trade. Yes, we could be reckless, but we weren't stupid.

A Dog's Breakfast

*D*ogs came and went. Not that we weren't fond of them. But they just didn't last long. It was either old age or behavioral issues that did them in. Except for one, they all came to us by chance. More than a few times they would be "shop dogs"; strays that had taken up residence in the factory where Dad worked. Some were old and their owners had had a change of circumstance. A couple of them were purebreds. But those seemed to be the biggest troublemakers. A collie, whose name I have forgotten, was chewing a round bone with a hole in its middle from one of Mom's pot roasts. The bone got stuck around the collie's long, narrow snout, locking its jaw shut.

Its normal bouncy persona took on a slow stumbling gait as it wandered the lawn in bewilderment. The collie's attempts to remove the bone were clumsy and un-dog-like. We couldn't help snickering at its efforts. Finally, Dad took a fine-tooth hand saw and we held the dog while he carefully sawed. Once free of the bone, the dog bounced back to its normal collie self and we were free to laugh out loud in its presence.

Another pure bred was a spitz; a breed most aptly named for its disposition. It was equally unfriendly to adults and children. It met the end of its short tenure with us when it broke loose and raided the neighbor's chicken coop for the second time.

The mixed-breed dogs fared better with us. They seemed to be less into themselves and more into us. One shaggy fellow named Duke was an aging shop dog with some spaniel features and an arthritic limp. He was docile, loving, and loyal and thought the Lawtons were the best humans a dog could have.

Come to think of it, we Lawtons were mongrels ourselves. Scotch-Irish-Italian. Protestant-Catholic. It seemed to me it might be easier for my city cousins to know who they were and where they belonged. Their parents were either both Italian and Catholic, or both non-Italian and Catholic, or both non-Italian and non-Catholic. I assumed they didn't feel different from the norm or incomplete when they went to church. They didn't have to feel like they had to choose between two extremes, nor did they have to worry constantly about the outlier's final destiny.

We were unlike our neighbors, who were mostly big-time, full-time dairy farmers. Dad worked in a factory full-time and as a small-time farmer part-time. It made me uneasy that we didn't fit neatly into any one slot or the other. Because it seemed other families, friends, and neighbors who surrounded us fit snuggly into theirs.

Polly and Her Entourage

Polly, Billy, Mom & Kathy, Buffalo,
New York, 1945

Lawton Kids on Mosher's Horse Duke, Scipio, 1947

Cousin Carmen, Kathy, Billy, Polly, Cousin Mary Elizabeth, Christmas 1948

Kathy and the Pee Wee Duck   *Polly and Kathy, Scipio, 1947*

A Close Shave

One day, when I was seven, I found myself wearing my Sunday dress and shoes but it wasn't Sunday. I was standing on a step stool beside a hospital bed. I was standing on my tiptoes in order to see and be seen by the stretched-out-flat occupant of the bed. My father. Usually, he scooped me up and twirled me around. But he wasn't his usual. He was weak. Could not even lift his hand. All he could do was meet my eyes with his, give a short smile, and whisper "Hi, Kathy." A tear slid out from the corner of his eye. It landed on the white sheet and spread into a small, gray circle.

I understood that his car had crashed into a telephone pole. I understood he had some smashed-up bones. I understood he was sick inside.

I didn't understand then that Polly, Billy, and I had been allowed to be hospital visitors because it was likely he would die. Apparently, we were there to encourage him to live, or to say goodbye. Even if I had been told he might die, I would not have understood "die" nor would I have accepted it. My father going away and never coming back? That was something that could never happen in my world.

The one thing I did understand about that day was that Dad's tear had not come from his pain, it had come from his heart.

After several weeks of hospital stay, Mom took care of Dad at home for a few more weeks and eventually he went back to work and eventually back to being my strong, healthy father. But that scene at the hospital bed, with Mom outside in the hallway crying and the nurses trying to comfort her, left a warning somewhere inside me. Perhaps the world was bigger than just me and what I was doing at any given moment. There were powers at work I knew nothing about. Could they be even stronger than my parents?

Out of Curiosity

On a sunny warm day, after Mom finished her morning housework, we'd eat lunch and then go off to visit one of our neighbors. In those early days, Mom didn't have a driver's license, therefore, our visiting was done on foot along the dirt roads. Dad would have been at work, and Polly was old enough to stay home on her own. Billy came with us at first, but most of the time it was me and Mom.

Lou and Stell Mosher were two of our favorite neighbors. Equally as dear, but a decade younger than the Moshers, was the brother-sister team of Isabell Baker and Tom Marshall. We could see their Cork Street farmhouse from our front windows if we looked kitty-corner toward the northeast.

Long before we moved to the neighborhood, Isabell's husband died leaving her his family's dairy farm to run. Her brother Tom resigned his lucrative job managing the prize dairy herd of the Theodore Roosevelt family of Oyster Bay, Long Island. The story goes that the tone of Tom's wardrobe, when he arrived at Isabell's Scipio farm, was ruled by an envious collection of classy silk shirts.

Isabell was tall with a sturdy build; wore her white hair combed back in a bun; and favored floral house dresses. Her smile seemed sweet and genuine; though Mom thought Isabell could be a bit nosy and liked to gossip.

Isabell collected lots of everything. So compacted was the landscape inside her glass-enclosed front porch that objects melded into an indistinguishable mass. A narrow path survived to usher us to the kitchen door. Inside, all kitchen surfaces were occupied by more stuff. Dust and dirt had difficulty finding inroads. Only Isabell knew what was where and why.

The rest of the house was cluttered, but cared for. Isabell had a story to go with each piece of antique furniture that dominated the rooms. Mom and I were avid listeners. Mom's interest was the current dollar value of a piece. I liked the story value of the people and places tied to the object. On the best visits we'd climb the steep, creaky stairs to view a recent acquisition and be immersed in the world of the dusty tales that clung to it.

A few times Isabell would force a tune from the keyboard of the massive organ in the living room. Pumping air into the behemoth turned into a sustained cardio workout as her alternating leg action drove the two large foot pedals. At the same time her sturdy fingers worked the keyboard. A hoarse tune, full of pompous reluctance bellowed forth. In its overpowering presence I swear I could make out a dour disapproving face that frightened me.

It was rare to find Tom in the house except for meals. Tom was trim, wiry, and a couple inches shorter than Isabell. His smile revealed a chipped front tooth and a warm honest heart. He was usually found in the milk barn, climbing the silo, or on his tractor in one of his fields; Blue coveralls, rugged work shirts, and a wide-brimmed farmer's hat became his adopted wardrobe. Even in humbled trappings, Tom still held a classy silk-shirt swagger.

On more than one Easter Sunday morning, in their best clothes, Isabell and Tom came to our house bringing candy for Polly and Billy. And for me, they brought a large, hollow, white egg made of hardened sugar. I needed both of my hands to hold it. Through its open window at one end I could see a miniature, 3D, panoramic Easter scene. White sugar bunnies, yellow sugar chicks, green sugar grass, brown sugar trees, and multicolored sugar tulips. Isabell and Tom beamed as my delight spilled around them. Now, as I think of that moment, I can see in their faces wistful memories of their own Victorian-era childhoods when they, too, held similar wonderous confections of springtime, hope, and love.

The miniature scale of the inhabitants and the crystal sparkle of the white sugar shell fascinated me for a couple of weeks. Then a white bunny disappeared, followed by a yellow chick. By the time the tulips became a colorful memory, Mom caught on to the cannibal and removed the egg from the shelf over my bed.

To the west of us on Mosher Road lived the Merritt, Murphy, Minde, and McArthur families; a pity, though, not in alphabetical order. When the McArthurs moved out, the Maines moved in. Some of these neighbors were older couples like my grandparents, almost always home and welcoming to drop-in company. And they had cookies.

After any one of these neighboring excursions Mom and I arrived home to the same scenario.

"Time for your nap, Kathy."

"I don't need a nap."

"Well, I do, now lie down and be quiet."

Mom took her role of a 1950s housewife to a professional level. She spent her long days excelling in cooking, baking, canning, freezing, cleaning, gardening, parenting, sewing, and generally adding her brand of stylish flair to our family life in Scipio. We, of course, took all of this for granted. Evenings, she relaxed reading *Better Homes and Gardens* or watching Bishop Fulton J. Sheen on TV. But these afternoon naps were a favorite of hers.

She laid on Dad's pillow, on his side of the bed, me on hers. And though it was *my* nap, she always fell asleep first. This left me bored and with time on my hands. Sometimes it was enough for me to listen to her rhythmic breathing and look over at her comforting form in house dress, and sometimes, when she had been too tired to remove it, her apron. I watched her sleep. She in one world. Me, in mine.

We lay atop the white chenille bedspread with its uniform lines of white puffy bumps that defied my persistent tugging to free them. I suppose if I were tired enough, sleep would claim me, but most of the time, I had to work at dozing off. When I tired of the tuft-freeing exercise, I started thinking of all the things I could be doing.

In church, I learned that my Guardian Angel (GA) sits on my right shoulder "to light and guard, to rule and guide" my every move. However, I had inherited the narrow-shouldered Lawton physique, as a result, space was limited and the slope precarious. GA proved to be a featherweight contender when it came to securing her perch. Often the Angel of Curiosity, like a sweaty roller-derby queen, gave GA a quick elbow to the ribs and sent her winging down to some dark place where GA would question her career choice.

Such was the case at nap time when Curiosity prompted me to sneak out of bed and go to the dresser and open a drawer or two.

If Mom ever woke during my excursions, I never knew it. In one drawer was Dad's white handkerchiefs, neatly folded white Fruit of the Looms, the scapular Mom had hung on his bed when he was in the hospital, and underneath all this, four, ring-shaped, rubbery things with a tiny picture of a lamb on the labels that were stretched across each of the rolled-up circles. I wanted to ask about them, but then Mom would have known I'd been snooping. When I learn to read, I thought, I could figure them out myself. In Mom's drawer were brassieres, panties, garters, nylon stockings, and two sets of worn-looking rosary beads. I wondered if the smallest one was hers when she was a little girl. But again, I couldn't ask.

The last stop on my snooping tour was the elegant dressing table with the tall, oval mirror and the drawers on either side that held all kinds of grown-up lady stuff: delicate hankies, silky scarves, and jewelry. I smoothed my hair with the silver-plated hairbrush that had belonged to one of my great-grandmothers, piled on strands of colorful beads, sprayed on some Evening In Paris, and felt grand and beautiful.

Dulled by the silence and the shade-darkened room, I'd head back to bed. The coil springs supporting the mattress had to be scaled with great deft less the squeaks wake Mom. Once there, I would lie flat on my stomach with my face on the bedspread. Then I would skooch down to the foot of the bed to slide my feet into the space between the mattress and footboard. My toes would start their rhythmic push that would rock the mattress just enough to rock me to sleep.

Whether it was me or Mom who woke first, I was always ready to bounce back into action. First, though, I had to go to the dressing table mirror and check my face for the funny pock marks inflicted on me by those round chenille tufts I had tortured earlier.

"Sh-Boom! Sh-Boom!"

"She's quiet. Sweet, but too shy for her own good." That could have been any two grown-ups who knew me, talking about me, while towering above me. In this case it was a well-meaning Aunt Mae and my well-meaning mother.

Their words were not a casual observation followed by a shrug of their shoulders. Indeed, if it was Mother, a teacher, or one of Mother's friends talking, disappointment tinged their words, sometimes disapproval. Various shades of alarm began to seep into the conversations that were always about me, but without me, even though I was right there. The tone of their words escalated from a mere pronouncement, to a diagnosis, and then to an indictment. What could I do?

I didn't know how to be anything other than me. My nature was to learn about new people and new places by observing. I needed to get a sense for the type of people they were. When walking into an unfamiliar home or store my top priority was taking in details. I wasn't rude. I'd say hello and answer questions. But if I didn't have a question of my own or an immediate need, why would I have to talk? What kid makes small talk anyway?

THE HOME BUREAU CREED.

TO MAINTAIN the highest ideals of home life; to count children the most important of crops to so mother them that their bodies may be sound, their minds clear, their spirits happy, and their characters generous:

To place service above comfort; to let loyalty to high purposes silence discordant notes; to let neighborliness supplant hatreds; to be discouraged never:

To lose self in generous enthusiasms; to extend to the less fortunate a helping hand; to believe one's community may become the best of communities; and to cooperate with others for the common ends of a more abundant home and community life:

This is the offer of the Home Bureau to the homemaker of today.

RUBY GREEN SMITH

When I went to stay with cousins during the summer, it took a few days to feel like I fit in. I remained quiet but shed a layer or two of shyness. When Mom and Dad came to pick me up at the end of my visit, aunts and uncles gave a report on my behavior. The word quiet was always part of it.

My report cards from school said I played well with others, what then, was the big deal?

Turns out everything in the 1950s was a big deal. And loud. It was all set in motion the same year I was born when the United States ended World War Two by dropping two atomic bombs. Boom! Boom! Just like that.

Boom! Went the U.S. economy as factories traded defense production for consumer goods. Boom! Boom! Went the crews of workers, earth movers, bridge builders, pavement layers, steelworkers, who among other things built the interstate highway system and the St. Lawrence Seaway. Both increased travel and commerce which put even more Boom! in the Boom! Prosperity loomed large and spawned the baby Boom! And televisions exploded into our living rooms bringing with them the whole loud messy world.

Turns out this disease I had, was part of an epidemic. "Inferiority complex" was its name. During the 1950s, it swept up all the inferior adults and children who were not outgoing, loud, aggressive, and extroverted.

Silver-tongued salesmen, bold, brassy entertainers, and boisterous business people–those were the icons of success in the 1950s. And it was imperative we all be boomingly successful.

No one had bothered to explain any of this to me. All I knew was that there was something wrong with me which I had no idea of how to fix. But Mom did.

She read *Good Housekeeping, Better Homes and Gardens, LIFE* magazine, and *Ladies Home Journal.* They encouraged her natural creativity and culinary skills. They entertained her with short stories, jokes, and cartoons. And with their pulse on postwar America, with its flourishing economy, its gung-ho attitude, and its technological advances, these publications reinforced her view that I was seriously flawed. She must have feared for me and my future and perhaps the negative impact my failure would have on her perceived success as a parent.

Another influence in Mom's life was her membership in the local Home Bureau group. They met once or twice a month in the vacated one-room schoolhouse near the corner of Mosher Road and Black Street. Formed in 1919, the Home Bureau was a New York State sister organization to the national Farm Bureau. The Farm Bureau was a collective voice for the business of farming. Home Bureau was an outreach from Cornell University to rural New York State women.

This self-described sisterhood of friends stated lofty ideals in a written creed and its own song. It was the perfect roadmap for homemakers of the 1950s who had, a few years earlier, been essential employees in wartime factories or served in World War Two quasi-military roles. Displaced by men reclaiming their prewar jobs, postwar standards urged women to not just revert to homemaking but be boomingly successful homemakers.

In this, the Home Bureau aligned. Primarily, these neighborhood meetings were a bright spot in Mom's limited rural social calendar. This did not prevent Mom and me from running afoul of the Bureau's creed.

A mother's responsibility, to paraphrase the Creed, was to consider children the most important crop. Children were mothered so their bodies may be sound, their spirits happy, their minds clear, and their characters generous. The "spirits happy" part clashed with the traits of my inferiority complex. I was doomed.

When I filled my alone time with my preferred silence, Mom thought I was sad and arranged playdates for me. Several were with Mary Lou; whose mother was a member of Mom's Home Bureau sisterhood group.

While learning flower arranging, needlepoint, or aluminum tray acid-etching, their conversations must have bristled with alarm for their two quiet and inferior daughters. Despite Mary Lou being three years older than me, she and her mom gathered me up a few times to spend the afternoon at their house. Two loners thrown together on a whim with nothing more in common than their quietness created quite the awkward nonstir.

One day we spent an hour boondoggling. The intensity of the task precluded conversation. On another visit, we toured Mary Lou's yard and barnyard, after which we sat under a tree in her front yard; each with our noses in separate books. Two oddities mirroring our shared disease.

Neither of us fussed over an occasional afternoon together, but neither of us minded when the visits stopped. No doubt our defeated mothers had reconvened over a Home Bureau lesson on menu-planning and pronounced their experiment a failure. No doubt they vowed to somehow or other remove the weeds of inferiority from this current crop.

Funny, now that I think about it, Dad never complained about my quiet ways. He would set me straight when I did something wrong or make a mistake. But with the basic me, he seemed at ease.

Leading a Lamb
to Slaughter

Scene of the Crime: W.T. Grant Co., Department Store, Genesee Street, Auburn, New York

Cast of Characters: Polly, Billy, Mother, and Kathy (sweet, innocent, unsuspecting Kathy)

The Setup: Mother shopping for fabric, thread, and notions. The Gang of Three slip from under her watchful gaze and by a stroke of mere luck they arrive at the candy counter.

The Inciting Incident: "Kathy, see those lollipops over there?"

"No, where?"

"Walk straight ahead. When your nose touches the glass, the lollipops will be right above your head. Reach up, take three, run back here. We'll let you have one, okay?"

I reached. I grabbed. I dashed. I caught up with Polly and Billy two aisles over in the lady's underwear department–large ladies. The huge panties hanging from the rafters were as long as I was tall and must have been meant to fit an elephant, because no lady could be that big. Could they? We removed the wrappers from the lollipops and basked in our sweet success.

Just then, fresh from the notions counter and with no notion of what we had been up to, the dark shadow of Moral Authority (MA) fell over the Lawton Gang of Three.

"Where did you get those lollipops?" Mother asked and accused in the same breath.

"Kathy took them from the candy counter."

"Did you, Kathleen Ann?"

"Uh huh."

Mother handed the notions to Polly, collared Kathy, and marched her down the aisle to the store manager. Polly and Billy followed behind, no doubt sharing a furtive look of triumph that summed up the situation:

1. The Brat's in trouble.

2. We put her there.

3. We've got candy.

4. High five. (Though in the 1950s it would have been an "A-OK" sign, with or without the wink of an eye.)

The voice of MA detailed my crime to the store manager. All eyes turned to me looking for shame and repentance.

"But they told me to do it."

"That doesn't matter. You never take anything that belongs to someone else," said (MA). "How much do we owe you?" she asked the manager. And she paid it.

As (MA) ruled the indoors, Dad's authority (DA) governed the outdoors. A week or two after the lollipop incident, I saw the two of them, Polly and Billy, slip around behind the barn. Trying to leave me out again, were they? As I crept up behind them, I saw smoke curling above their heads.

"Hey, what are you two doing?"

They wheeled around in shock. I tried to make sense of them holding a smoking cigarette; something only adults were allowed to do. They sh-sh-shushed me, then forced me to take a drag making me an accessory after the fact. Dad must have heard our voices or me gagging on the smoke, because he was next to join the secret meeting. We were immediately marched into the house where both MA and DA combined forces. For the next four hours the two of them directed our activities which consisted of: sweep the floor, dust the furniture, pick up that tiny piece of fluff in the middle of the rug, dispose of it properly. This was accompanied by parental commentary; "stop pouting, it doesn't matter that you didn't know what they were doing, you smoked anyway."

This part of my childhood coincided with a popular phrase from the Superman comic books that neatly summed the Lawton's approach to daily living. While Superman defended "truth, justice, and the American Way" he never showed up when I needed to know which side of truth and justice I was on. No one told me that truth and justice are moving targets. But in the course of my being a good child and staying safe, I sensed the wisdom of being one step ahead of the shifting bull's-eye.

Along with cigarettes and stolen candy, there was at least one more thing that we kids weren't allowed. Swear words. We were used to hearing Dad's *damns, hells,* and others too colorful to mention. Mom rarely swore. But when she did, she swore in Italian. *Jesu Christo.* As though we couldn't figure that out!

Back then, yes, the pope was Catholic. And Italian. So, I figured Mom and other Italian-speaking swearers got a free pass while it was a mortal sin for the rest of us.

Barking Up the Wrong Tree

"*H*and me that big wrench, will you?" Dad asked.

I pawed around in the toolbox and handed over what I hoped was a wrench. Dad's tractor had to be fixed before he could rake the rest of the hayfield. Tom Marshall and his hay baler were to arrive the next morning at daybreak. Frustrated, hot, and racing against time, Dad needed help. I had been the only kid in sight, plus I had two hands. I got the job.

"Would you get me a cold drink of water?" Ah, something in my comfort zone.

When I returned with a jar of ice water, Dad's face was dripping sweat. The air bubble surrounding Dad and the ailing tractor was dripping blue with all of the "goddamnits" and "sonsabitches" he had offered up in my brief absence.

From Dad's mumblings, I gathered the problem could be easily fixed. But getting to the problem was the problem. The nut withholding access to the problem refused to move no matter how Dad tried to persuade it.

"Hand me that rag." Then, a second time, much louder, "Kathy, hand me that rag."

I jumped to attention pulling my mind back to my job. It had wandered off, wondering why those metal things were called nuts, when they had nothing in common with hickories or chestnuts or any other category of nut I knew of.

"Pay attention," I told myself. Dad's temper could take off like a spiral-spinning firework whose shriek grew louder as it blasted higher and faster. I did not want to be the one who lit it up.

A strange, blue car that had seen better days drove into the driveway. It was a Saturday. Chances were good, then, that these were Seventh Day Adventists fresh from their weekly service. Usually, it would have been Mom who greeted them at the door telling them politely, "we are firm Roman Catholics and have no need of your message."

She would allow them a half-sentence more of grace time, then she'd spat her final words through clenched teeth.

"I said we are not interested."

They would slip a pamphlet into her hand and step back. She'd close the door with a bang, leaving no doubt she was, indeed, firm in her faith. Mom always destroyed the pamphlet within seconds lest we sin by reading anything outside our faith.

Truth be told, she lied. We were not all firm Roman Catholics. Like I said, Dad had come from a long line of Protestants. He had been baptized Catholic only in order to marry Mom and save her from excommunication. Except for the odd Christmas Eve or Easter Sunday, Dad limited his church-going to weddings and funerals. Even on those occasions he seemed restless, distracted, out of place. Whatever his beliefs were or were not, he never tried to dissuade Mom or any of us from being Catholics.

Once, I point-blank asked him why he didn't go to our church with us.

"I don't like all the mumbo-jumbo," he said, referring to the Mass being said in Latin. That was the extent of his spoken opinion on the church.

Dad had made a solemn promise that his children would be raised as Catholics and his word was his bond.

Mom labeled him a heathen. I learned all about heathens while learning about the French missionary, St. Isaac Jogues. He had been martyred while converting the Iroquois to Catholicism and our church was named for him. Native Americans, who resisted conversion to Christianity, were labeled "heathens." Therefore, I deduced, the same certain damnation that would have befallen any unsaved Indian, would befall my father as well.

It seemed so damn unfair. Why would God be all-loving and all-merciful just to Catholics? That thought gnawed at me. Surely God would know a good Indian when He saw one whether converted or not. And surely, He would know my Dad was an extra-good heathen, wouldn't He?

On this Saturday in July, Mom had been in the kitchen and unaware of the door-to-door evangelism that was about to take place in our driveway. A man about Dad's age, and two younger women, stepped out of the car and walked over to the tractor.

Nodding to me, but addressing Dad, the man said, "Good day, sir. The Lord has given us a good day, wouldn't you agree?"

Dad did not raise his eyes from his task, but in a firm voice told the callers that he had his own religion. He had no need to hear anything further and couldn't they see he had this tractor trouble to attend to. Undeterred, the man asked a series of questions and each time provided his own biblical answer because Dad remained silent and focused on the problem. Five minutes into this one-way conversation, the man said, "What day do you keep your Sabbath, brother?"

That did it. Dad threw his wrench to the ground and turned to face the callers who had moved to within arm's reach of him.

"Jesus Christ! I told you I have my own religion. Now, goddammit, get the hell outta here and leave me alone."

Well, at least it wasn't me who lit the wick.

In their panic to flee, the trio burst the delicate air bubble they had crowded into with Dad and the tractor. A few of the floating "goddamnits" were sucked into the air current that followed close at their heels. They took refuge in their car and were soon speeding west on Mosher Road. In their wake, they raised a hellish cloud of dust. As the road dust settled, so, too, did the dozen mangled curse words as they floated self-satisfied, to the ground.

Dad sighed, picked up his wrench, and locked its jaws around the nut. On his first try, the nut gave way and turned like it had always meant to. Speechless, he and I looked at each other for a few seconds. I saw a sparkle in Dad's eyes that jumped to the corners of his mouth. A wide grin broke out all over his face. I let loose the grin I had been holding back. Mom came on the scene just as we burst out laughing.

"What's the joke?" she asked.

"I found a quick way to get rid of the Seventh Day Adventists," Dad told her, turning back to address the problem.

"Did you tell them we were Catholic?" she asked, looking first at him, then at me.

"No," he said. "I just told them I had my own religion and they left."

"Is that right, Kathy?" She wanted to know.

"Uh huh."

Had I told her the whole truth, I would have had to take the Lord's name in vain. Then both I and "that heathen" would have been in trouble. I felt that Dad had had enough for one day. The hay had yet to be raked, he was hot, tired, and sweaty. But more to the point, some nuts are just too hard to crack.

Hung Out to Dry

A suggested schedule for full-time housewives of the 1950s:

Wash on Monday
Iron on Tuesday
Mend on Wednesday
Market on Thursday
Clean on Friday
Bake on Saturday
Rest on Sunday

It was one of those steamy summer mornings, probably a Monday, when boredom seized me and wouldn't let go. Desperate, I dragged myself to the cool basement where Mom and her wringer-washer might provide action and entertainment.

When I entered the scene of the action, the agitator was sloshing hot sudsy water and our laundry back and forth in the tub. The sloshing action filled the cool, damp air with the scent of Tide's promise of the "cleanest clean under the sun!" Mom pushed a lever down and the water and suds spilled into the drain. Then she put the hose in the tub, turned the faucet on and filled the tub with cold rinse water. The gears, knobs, levers, and switches were Mom's domain. I admired the confident, fluid style with which she managed them.

I sat on the cellar steps, elbows on knees, chin in hands, watching the process, waiting for the sequence to get to my role, if I wanted it. Today, I wanted it. Once the rinse water emptied into the drain, I grabbed the clothes basket and took my place behind the washing machine. Mom picked a sopping wet towel from the tub and fed it into the front of the wringer; two rollers, one atop the other, both spinning inward. This spin action caught the towel, squeezed the water back into the tub, and moved the flattened towel along and into my hands. I then placed the towel into the basket and turned to catch the next item of laundry.

For some reason, the wringing process appealed to me. The wringer itself seemed like a hungry mouth, grabbing hold of the clothes, wringing the hell out of them, and spitting them out the other side, flat, like a jeering tongue. I liked that it deformed our familiar clothes into comical shapes. Billy's undershirt wrung to fit a chest three inches wide by three feet tall. Polly's underpants, put through the wringer sideways, made wide enough for a hippo's hips, but a hippo who was flat as a pancake.

But that wringer had a split personality; one of which was diabolical. It might pretend to mistake loose apron strings or a woman's long hair strands for clothing and clamp its jaws shut and draw them in. Though this hadn't happened at our house, there was an incident where it grabbed Mom's thumb and mangled it until she was able to hit the off button and then, one-handed, released the lever to spread the rollers apart. There was no blood or broken bones, but there was some serious bruising and some healthy fear instilled in all of us.

Once the load of wash had been put through the wringer and placed in the basket, we took it outside to hang on our backyard clothesline. In winter, on blustery days the laundry dried on clotheslines in the cellar. But if it were a crisp, sunny winter day, they went outside to the backyard clotheslines, where in their semidry state, they froze into flat, stiff clothing for life-sized, cut-out paper dolls but missing the folding tabs.

During the summer, Mom and the clothesline figured into our Cold War play. If I were an American spy crouching behind the red currant bush, Barbie was my collaborator, stationed across the yard behind the corner of the barn. Halfway between us was Mom. To the outside world, she appeared to be an ordinary housewife hanging laundry on the clothesline. Unbeknown to all, including herself, Agent Mom was providing the clandestine communication that fueled our action.

Her use of the newfangled spring clothespins identified Agent Mom as a Russian spy, or double agent. We didn't know which. We had broken her code. We deciphered that one white, flat sheet hung horizontally by two clothes pins, followed by a blue towel, signaled to Agent Mom's invisible comrade, that she had hidden the stolen documents in a rented locker at the bottom of the black walnut tree. Had there been four clothespins on that one sheet, it would have meant to proceed only under cover of darkness. Knowing we were safe to proceed we did, indeed, proceed with stealthy moves to throw the enemy off our trail. We proceeded to recover said documents. Then we proceeded back to intercept more coded messages.

Had there been three pair of ladies' nylons hanging on the east end of the line, it would have told us the Russians knew our whereabouts and were in hot pursuit. But, instead, it was two men's briefs followed by two boy's briefs meaning the Russians were following a false lead and we had time to halt our mission and proceed to the kitchen for lemonade.

But on those summer days, when it was just Mom and me and the wash, I proceeded to help Agent Mom pin and then unpin the laundry from the clothesline. When it came to folding those sheets, Mom and I each took two corners, stretched it out full length and taut, folded it in half, and in half again, tugged it taut, then performed the square dance step of forward and back. Four steps forward, four hands meet in the middle, hand off corners to my partner, bow and pick up the folded end, two steps back, tug it taut, two steps forward, hand off all to my partner. Do-si-do your partner (optional) and start again.

While drying on the line, the cotton fibers of the bed linens trapped the best of the farm fresh Scipio air. Reluctant to succumb to bedtime, as is any kid in summer, I was quick to surrender to slumber once wrapped in the *Eau de Parfum* known as Scipio's Sunshine which exuded the floral essence of mother-love and the earthy base note of well-being.

Though not in the limelight she desired, Mom's 1950s life was full of large and small tasks done with careful attention and according to her own schedule. She infused daily projects with a determined and creative zest while demonstrating mindfulness decades before it was to become a trendy spiritual practice. Mom was the safe and sure presence, who taught me to lean into any task and feel my own importance.

Yes, there's nothing sweeter nor as fleeting as a mother's tug at the other end of a fresh laundered bed sheet.

All Our Ducks
in a Row

Our spy games mimicked the Cold War dramas we watched on TV. *I Led Three Lives,* was a weekly series based on the true story of Herbert Philbrick. He was, first, a white-collar worker, then secretly infiltrated the Communist party, and then secretly became a double agent, reporting to the FBI. Sure, sometimes I was lost and confused in the twisting and turning plots of his multiple lives. But I could tell good from evil. America was Good. Communism, Russians, and the USSR were evil. And Russia was on its way to devour America.

This chilling dichotomy was further impressed upon us in our classrooms. We watched filmstrips showing thick black arching arrows, Communism's octopus-like arms, descending over the helpless shoulders of eastern Europe. And because Russia, too, had the atomic bomb, the fear of Russian attack on the Free World came at us from TV, radio, newspapers, magazines and, yes, more filmstrips in the classroom.

Mrs. Maroney was writing this week's second-grade spelling words on the blackboard. The rhythmic click of the chalk revealed the next letter of an unfamiliar word that I copied onto my lined paper. Then, a louder, more demanding click—and the PA system snapped to life spewing a short blast of static from the speaker above my head.

"Attention, please. This is an air raid drill," came Principal Gazely's serious voice.

A second later the air raid siren sound blasted from the speaker and soaked into the nooks and crannies of the classroom. In seconds, Mrs. Maroney, all thirty of my classmates and I were underneath our desks, our heads covered by our crossed arms. This exercise we'd learned from a filmstrip featuring a cartoon character, Bert the Turtle, and an officious male narrator with a clipped, nasal, newsreel-type voice. Bert was a confident goody-two-shoes turtle, who knew what to do in each and every emergency thrown at him; especially when seeing an atomic bomb flash. Duck and Cover! His answer to everything.

We were bright enough kids to clue into a turtle being the most effective character for the duck and cover message. But in true over-the-top 1950s subliminal style, Bert (not Burt) sported a white clergyman's collar, a black bow tie, and a Brody-style metal military helmet from World Wars One and Two.

A team of ad men, I'm guessing, were hired to slick-up Bert's appearance. Wearing identical horned rim glasses and brush cuts, they worked late into the night until they chose the name Bert. Short for the male name Bertrand, which meant bright one. Male, of course, signified authority. The clergy collar shouted trustworthiness. The black bow tie was the symbol of a booming CEO's attire. And the Brody helmet marched into our tiny, dark brains to ignite thoughts of military might. We were in a war, after all.

From under my desk, I lifted my elbow to peek around at other kids peeking around. We were a tense and twitchy herd of turtles. I noticed that next to Mrs. Maroney, who'd ducked and covered beneath her wide oak teacher's desk, there was just enough room to fit one ducked and covered second grader. Considering our skimpy student desks left us exposed on three sides, I was probably not the only conniving kid thinking when it's the real thing, that oak desk would be the turtle shell for me.

Three short blasts of the siren and it was all clear. Un-duck, un-cover. Back to spelling.

By the time I advanced to Mrs. Haine's third-grade class, the drill had been changed to exit the classroom and go into the hallway (no windows), and assume the duck and cover position against the walls.

The confusing part came when we were shown filmstrips of actual atomic blasts using real buildings and human dummies. Everything got vaporized and sucked up into a mushroom cloud. How then was a student desk, a teacher's desk, or our arms covering our heads going to keep us safe from Russian bombs? Bert, at least, had a helmet.

The U.S. Civil Defense Commission advised fallout shelters be built to escape the radiation, should we be lucky enough to survive the initial blast. But there were no fallout shelters built in Scipio.

Scared? Yes, I was.

Terrified? Yes, I was.

But I could do nothing more than look to the two adults who kept me safe so far. Since they didn't build a bomb shelter, I guess Mom and Dad accepted the risk of us being vaporized. They didn't seem panicked, just watchful and wary.

During this time, they also kept up to date with the eighty-four days of televised congressional hearings led by Sen. Joseph McCarthy. They explained to me that he was accusing people in government, the military, and the entertainment industry of being Communist operatives and un-American sympathizers. By their comments while watching the hearings or by talk at the dinner table, I picked up on their disagreement with Sen. McCarthy. Polly, a teenager, was able to engage in these dinner table discussions too. The general Lawton consensus that I absorbed along with my supper, was that the hearings were a witch hunt. Mere finger-pointing by the likes of Senator McCarthy was enough to get innocent people blackballed.

"Blackballed" was one of Dad's union terms which I knew was painful to us on a personal level. Grandpa Lawton, Dad had explained once, was a union organizer, "back when it was dangerous to be one; it could get you killed. He would go to secret meetings held at night-time in barns way out in the country."

The union organizers of that era laid the foundation leveling the playing field between labor and management. Fair wages were one issue. Safer working conditions, another. Local newspapers from the early 1900s had daily reports of numerous industrial accidents. The reporters of the day spared none of the gruesome details of severed limbs, heads, or torsos.

Grandpa worked in the iron industry and became the treasurer of Syracuse Local 80, Iron Moulder's Union. When the unions called a strike in 1919 and early 1920, the strikers lined up weekly on Grandpa Lawton's lawn to draw their strike pay.

"Big, burly tough-types," said my dad, "wearing the grass on the front lawn down to nothin'. But they treated us kids real nice, because of who my father was."

But once the strike was settled, Grandpa was labeled a union agitator by the industry's management and was blackballed, meaning no one in the industry would hire him. This was a different form of Iron Curtain and it descended around Grandpa costing him his livelihood, the family home, and a comfortable village lifestyle.

Grandpa reinvented himself as a farmer, moving the family to hilly farmland in northern Cayuga County, where they raised vegetables; carting them by truck to the Syracuse produce market. Dad and his siblings went from a comfortable, middle-class, small-town lifestyle to a hard-scrabble, farm-kid reality. Things worsened as Grandpa developed tuberculosis, most likely from the toxic air he breathed while working in the iron foundries. He died at the age of fifty-one years just before the stock market crash of 1929 and the Depression years that followed.

No wonder Dad, and therefore the rest of us, didn't like finger-pointers and greedy people who used their power to ruin other people's lives. Though Grandpa Lawton had taken a big hit for his role in the union, Dad, looked up to him.

Riding home one day in the farm truck, Grandpa Lawton and Dad, who'd just become a teenager, passed a neighboring farm. Out in a field bordering the road, they saw a group of mentally disabled people the farmer had hired from a nearby institution. They were working in the freezing rain. Some had no shoes and none were wearing anything more than ragged pants, shirts, and dresses.

Arriving home, Grandpa went into the house, came out with his rifle and he and Dad drove back to the neighboring farm. Grandpa found the farmer and with rifle in hand, ordered him to get those people out of the field and make sure they got warm and dry. Then Grandpa threatened the farmer with a call to the county sheriff if he ever saw or heard of any mistreatment in the future.

I wish I knew more about Grandpa Lawton. His memory was shrouded in more silence and secrets than facts. But through these selective stories, Dad passed on to us Grandpa Lawton's principles of fairness and compassion. Unspoken, but understood, is the courage it took to put his beliefs into action.

A Different Kettle
of Fish

During summer, my siblings, our many cousins, and I were moved around among each other's homes like peas in the old shell game. The shells were labeled Auburn, Village of Cayuga, and Scipio. Billy went to cousin Carmen's. Polly went to Aunt Mae's or to the Sperduti's. Some years I went to the Colella's. There, with my cousins Mary and Gerard, I roller skated on Auburn's sidewalks—a novelty for a paving-deprived Scipio kid.

Some summers, I went to the lakeside village of Cayuga and faded seamlessly into the thirteen Lawton cousins who lived there. We didn't have blocks in Scipio; therefore, the village conveniences were an eye-opener. With two, four, or six of my cousins at any one time, I walked the three village blocks to Cayuga Lake for swim lessons. With the lake near, my cousins swam daily and qualified for the advanced classes. My frequent but sporadic trips to the lake from Scipio required a car and driver. With no previous swim lessons, I couldn't perform the strokes and floats they asked of me. I got stuck in the beginner's group with younger kids learning the basics. My one clear memory is holding onto the dock, kicking in unison with the "babies" and looking around to find comfort in the familiar faces of my cousins.

The village corner store was only a two-block walk from my cousins' house. The Lawton kids were on a first-name basis with the owner behind the counter. I envied their daily access to Creamsicles, Necco Wafers and Bazooka bubble gum.

Concealed within this mass of Lawton cousins, I dared poach apples from the acres of orchard behind their house. The owner, I was told, was a mean, crotchety farmer, who scared the bejesus out of the neighborhood kids. More than once we had to hightail it out of the orchard when we heard his gunshots. If my cousins were telling the truth, he was not firing in the air.

Another week, I might stay at Aunt Mae's house in Auburn. Aunt Mae was Dad's only sister. She and their youngest brother, Charles, were both soft gingers, not the vivid fiery variety. Dad and Uncle Jim had dark hair and brown eyes. Aunt Mae was soft-spoken, and refined. Her hardly-there freckles were a signal of a gentle nature.

Her son, my cousin Paul, was an only child. He was nice to me even though he was the same age as Polly. Most of our interactions were saying hi and goodbye when we passed each other as he was leaving for his part-time job or his friends' houses. While waiting for Uncle Gilbert to come home for supper, Aunt Mae showed me how to set a stylish table. I helped wash dishes in the kitchen sink with Aunt Mae instructing me in her soft, clipped speech, "I find cold water discourages the suds." She was my 1950s Martha Stewart.

My time spent with Aunt Mae was a bite of tasteful culture. We listened to band concerts in Auburn's Hoopes Park, afterward, topping off the evening with an ice cream cone. Or we drove around Skaneateles Lake stopping for lunch at a ritzy Skaneateles village inn; one with white tablecloths and real linen napkins. Sometimes we visited one of her fancy friends' lake cottage that seemed more city house than lake cottage.

Aunt Mae was at ease in her city lifestyle and it suited her well. While I admired her and enjoyed my week's visit, I was glad to slip back into my plainer, more down-to-earth Scipio lifestyle where I didn't feel I was "putting on airs." Mom and Aunt Mae were always good friends, but Mom would scoff at Aunt Mae's city lifestyle and social standing. But it was clear to me Mom would have liked the same for herself.

Other summers I visited my Fiduccia relatives: Aunt Betty, Uncle Tony, and cousins Michael, Carmen, and Mary Elizabeth. They lived on Richardson Avenue in Auburn.

Mary 'lisbeth, as we called her, knew a maid at one of the mansions on nearby South Street. She knocked on the mansion's kitchen door at the back, spoke to the maid asking permission to show me the park-like backyard. We walked along paved paths past fruit trees, flower gardens, and ponds; one with a fountain and goldfish. A gardener knelt at the border of one flower bed. He looked up at us and smiled but never stopped hand-trimming the lush grass threatening to step in where it didn't belong.

Back home again, I daydreamed about living in such a mansion. My imaginary lives, staged in the barn's haymow, included me as a rich lady with a lavish wardrobe attending society balls.

But in those city spells with relatives, I felt like an imposter. I didn't want the city strangers walking or driving by me to think I belonged there. I wanted them to know I was just visiting.

No matter the season, nor the venue, child's play in the 1950s was a full-time unstructured job. When rural life didn't provide a playmate for me it was up to me to keep myself occupied. Influenced by my storybooks and television programs, any day's adventure might showcase me as a cowgirl, Indian princess, teacher, mother to my dolls, famous singer, and/or Sky King's niece, Penny. No one in my make-believe world thought I was too quiet and shy. In fact, I was as brave and courageous and talkative as anyone on television. My pretend world was wild and crammed full. Sometimes it overflowed into real life and got me into trouble for daydreaming.

Despite Mom's worry about my quietness, there were times when I had exhausted my imagination and craved another kid's company. Even if that kid was my stupid brother.

No Stone Unturned

"Billy, Mom said I could play whatever you and Gary are playing?" I lied.

"What? Have you got rocks in your head?" was his reply.

I gave him my dirtiest look and stomped off to get Mom's permission to begin the mile-long walk along dirt roads to Barbie's house. Mom phoned Barbie's mom who sent Barbie to meet me halfway.

"Don't forget to call when you get there," Mom said. "And hang up after the first ring," she added, because back then it was a long-distance call to just about anywhere past the four other households on our "party line."

As soon as I reached the bottom of our hill and turned south onto Cork Street, it was like a spell had been cast upon me and I entered into some other dimension. Suddenly I couldn't resist any of them. Glistening rocks reflected sunlight directly into my eyes and mesmerized me into doing their will.

"Pick me up, child. Put me in your pocket."

Then, colorful stones sweet-talked me until I was spellbound and their wishes became my commands.

"Be a dear kind child and carry us home with you. We'll stay on your shelf–won't be any trouble."

Tiny pebbles pleaded with me to pluck them from obscurity. By the time my svelte seven-year-old frame arrived at Barbie's house it was the shape and size of a Sumo wrestler; albeit a very short one.

But that day paled in comparison to the day I became a serious collector; the day Dad brought home a shiny red Radio Flyer wagon. I already owned the perfect accessory: an older brother to pull it. What I didn't have was a way to make him do it. But as fate would have it, a few days later Billy and I were the only company each of us had.

We were playing in Tom Marshall's pasture. Billy mucked around in the creek filling his bucket with water and tadpoles. I wandered the pasture picking wildflowers. Then, I stumbled on it. A dazzling, pure white rock with silver veins and glittery bumps that I knew in my heart of hearts were diamonds. This was huge! Boiling with excitement, I ran back to the creek.

"Please, please, please, Billy, I have to have it, I have to, I have to. Help me get it home."

Jumping up and down, I begged him over and over and over again. Apparently, one too many times. In an instant I was shocked silent. A cold, slimy bucketful of frog eggs hit the crown of my head, oozed down through my hair, leached onto my face, and slithered all the way to my shoes.

Crying and cursing, I ran off toward home to get the slime off me and to get my brother in trouble. Big trouble.

Billy ran after me. He must have realized the consequences of me telling my story first.

"Hold up," he said grabbing my arm and stopping me still. "Honest, I'm sorry," he spit out in the spaces between his giggles.

We both knew he wasn't sorry. He had enjoyed each gelatinous, if not premeditated, minute. Given the chance, he would do it all over again. Naturally I rejected his flimsy act of contrition.

Quick thinking then led him to invent the story he would tell Mom that would keep us both out of trouble. Kathy slipped and fell into the creek. The end.

I pretended to think about this for a moment. While he held his breath, I formed my strategy. I would accept both his stupid apology and his fabricated story, but on one condition.

Later that afternoon, in fulfillment of that one condition, Billy, the Red Flyer, the shovel, and I marched out of the Lawton driveway, down the hill, under the electric fence, and around all the cow flops. By the time we reached my intended quarry, the wagon was already half full of buttercups, daisies, sticks, and a tree frog a certain brother must have added when I wasn't looking.

Billy dug and dug, sweat and swore, and when unearthed, the rock was almost the same size as the Red Flyer. It took all our might, and many tries, to get it into the wagon. Billy pulled and I pushed the new-but-creaking wagon through the pasture onto the road and up the hill.

"Okay, where do you want it?" asked Billy, sweat dripping from his forehead.

"Right here on the edge of the lawn next to the road," I said.

"What for?"

"Because."

Back there in the pasture while Billy had been digging up this rock, I had been surveying and mapping. Upon safe placement of this first specimen I asked, " When do we go back for the others?"

"Never! This is it, you slimeball sister."

"I wonder," I said with eyes rolled skyward and fingertips drumming my chin, "what Mom would do if she were to find out you slimed me on purpose."

I could read the words of Billy's internal dialog as if they were rolling in flashing neon across his forehead.

"I'm going to kill her. No, Mom might get mad. And what the heck, if roles were reversed, I'd be blackmailing Kathy. Heck, I do it all the time."

But aloud he said only, "Okay, I'll go. But, tomorrow."

Within a week I had an inventory of six large rocks all in a row on the front lawn. Who could have argued with me for putting the biggest price tag on my diamond rock?

"Now I'm sure you've got rocks in your head." (Billy again.) "Who's going to buy these stupid rocks?"

"People who drive by," I answered with confidence.

Day, after summer day, I kept the grueling hours of a serious retailer. After a week of no one stopping, I added a lemonade stand. A car slowed down and I thought I had a customer. But it was the mailman who smiled, waved, and delivered the mail all in one nonstop motion.

I closed shop early. I was bored and discouraged. I headed to the barn to play school. Maybe nobody but me wanted the rocks. What if my brother was right for once? Was selling rocks a stupid idea? Was something else wrong other than my quiet and shy disease? Maybe I did have rocks in my head!

Birds of a Feather

There are certain skills you learn, living on a dirt road, that could be passed off to the unsuspecting as clairvoyance. Heck, sometimes I even convinced myself.

The moment I grew tall enough to see out the kitchen window, Billy gleefully stepped aside. It became my job, then, to watch for the school bus. My line of surveillance paralleled the road running west. It struck out across our lawn, skipped over the vegetable garden, traversed our hayfield, burrowed through a hole in the hedgerow and arrived at the far end of the neighbor's cornfield— almost a mile straight away from the window. That's where linear perspective made its point–a pinpoint. And that was my window of opportunity on Mosher Road.

On springtime mornings, when the road was still wet and muddy and the trees only budding, my eyes locked onto that pinpoint to grab the split-second of blazing yellow.

"Bus is coming," I would sing out. Those words, like a conductor's baton, set off a symphony.

Billy's arm extended like a slide trombone to toss his comic book down. From somewhere a trumpet proclaimed Polly beautiful and she, at last, withdrew from the mirror. Like a cello's bow I glided forward to grab my jacket and smoothly back to grab my Dale Evans lunchbox. Each of us in turn embraced our mother then twirled out of her arms while holding our waltz-type postures. We swept out the front door in three-quarter time.

At the edge of the lawn the tempo changed and we marched single file to a Sousa beat all the way down the driveway. The bus door opened with an accordion's wide, toothy grin, sucked us up with its bellows, and squeezed shut behind us. The drums roared! The cymbals crashed! Shouts of *Bravo!* filled the air. And I, the conductor, folded into a graceful bow.

That describes a morning when I was paying attention. If I day-dreamed and missed my cue, our dash for the bus looked more like a crazed and disheveled polka troupe that had drunk long and hard from the barrel before rolling it out.

On yet another morning at my watch-post I duly announced, "bus is coming."

"How do you know?" challenged a sleep-over friend standing at my side.

"Well, I just know. Sort of like magic," I lied, my pinpoint secret preserved. Her look of awe and her stunned silence told me I had hooked my first big fish.

My job got easier as May and June baked the road dry. The field corn grew to obscure that pinpoint. But, then I had dust on my side.

A little poof meant a car. A big poof was what I was looking for. But one morning the milk truck was running late and raised a solid cloud of dust all the way up the road to the neighbor's dairy barn. Next thing I knew the bus was out front honking its horn, and Polly, dying of embarrassment, threw me dirty looks all the way down the driveway. Beautiful never happened for her that day.

During summer vacation I honed my prognostication skills with car and truck traffic. Well, what there was of it. The bakery delivery truck was a twice-a-week regular. When the gravel hit its speeding floorboards, it sounded like a giant popcorn popper on wheels. And it always came in the morning about an hour before lunch. One Tuesday summer morning, the Lone Ranger (me) and Tonto (my city cousin staying the week) had just rounded up some cattle rustlers out in our pasture. Suddenly, The Lone Ranger turned Silver on his heels and galloped toward the house.

"Bakery truck is coming," I yelled behind me.

"How you know, Kemosabe?" came Tonto's response.

"I can smell the cookies," I lied. "Sort of like magic."

Now on Friday of that same week, when the popcorn popper was about half a mile away, Tonto was straddling two of the four horses of a runaway stagecoach. Suddenly, she dropped to the ground and out of character.

"Run," she shouted. "I can smell cookies and they're getting closer!"

I'd just had my first lesson in humility. Sort of like reeling in the "big one" only to find out what you've hooked, instead, is your own pant leg.

In the summer that I turned eight, I'd set up a classroom in the hayloft of our barn. I could be teaching addition to my students and still monitor traffic outside. I heard the car start to slow down when it came even with the hickory tree, a sure sign it was stopping for us. I went on teaching though, because it didn't sound like any car I knew. Too early for my dad to be home from work, not a bakery day, didn't come from Barbie's direction, and relatives only visited on weekends. Probably it was somebody lost or selling something. My class moved on to subtraction. But shortly into the lesson I heard my mother call . . . "Kaaaathy!"

I warned my class to behave as I left the classroom and started for the stairs. But the dangling rope at the edge of the haymow dared me. I morphed from teacher to Tarzan. My feet pushed me off the edge, the rope swung me out, my hands let go, and the loose straw pile below caught me gently and bounced me to my feet. Yes! Life was a nonstop adventure and who knew what the next moment would hold?

My eyes adjusted from the dim barn light to the bright outdoors. Who was that mysterious lady talking to my mother? From way across the lawn I could tell she was a city lady. As I neared them, I heard her bracelets jingle when her hand moved to shield the sun from her eyes. While I stood next to my mother listening to them talk about our neighbors, a July breeze rippled the silky blue skirt of the lady's fancy dress, sending small waves in all directions. I thought I smelled Lily of the Valley. She was the prettiest lady I'd ever seen.

"Kathy, this is Miss Laurel. Her family used to live in our house. When she was a little girl her father built the little stone house and its rock garden. Would you take her down the road to see it?"

About two feet high and a replica of an English or Irish country cottage it had been built on-site out of fieldstone and concrete. Scattered remnants of tulips, daffodils, and Lily of the Valley were ghostly reminders of a perennial rock garden. We called it either the Elf House or the Fairy House. It fit the bill for any structure our childhood dramas required. An old west bank that we robbers were casing, the hiding place for pirates' treasure, or a Cold War safe house where Russian spies were holed up. Curiosity sparked us to chip away at the wooden-slat door to see what was inside. But solid cement let us go no further.

Miss Laurel took my hand and teetered down the dirt road in her high-heeled city shoes. As we walked, she told me she lived in California, taught second grade, and would soon be getting married. When we reached the rock garden, she walked slowly around the little stone house, touching it with her hands. Then she bent down and picked up a small flat rock.

"May I take this rock with me, Kathy?" she asked. "It will help me remember my father and this special place." I nodded yes.

As she took my hand to walk back up the road, I looked up at her face and saw tears dribbling down her cheeks. She didn't say anything after that until we reached the edge of our yard.

"Kathy, are you selling these rocks?" she asked.

"Well, I'm trying to." I said. "But my brother Billy thinks it's stupid."

She took her time looking and touching each rock, especially the diamond rock.

"Well, I don't think it's stupid. I can't carry them back to California on the plane, but if I could, I would buy all of them. They are special. You remind me of myself when I was your age." Her tears started falling again, but faster.

She backed her car out of the driveway and onto the road. She smiled at me and waved "goodbye" then drove off. But she didn't hurry like the bakery truck or the milk truck. The soft thumps from the gravel and the lazy way the dust rose up over the cornfield told me she was taking her time.

I went back into the barn and climbed the stairs to my classroom. I walked toward the blackboard, this time, on tiptoes like I was wearing high-heeled city shoes. And when I chalked the subtraction lesson on the board, my imaginary bracelets jingled like little bells.

I never bothered to tell Billy about Miss Laurel and the rocks. He would have said she was just as crazy as I was. It was good enough for me to know that somebody as attractive, smart, and grown up as Miss Laurel felt the same way I did. And whether you lived far away in California or right here in Scipio, having rocks in your head was A-OK.

But rocks smothering your healthy lawn was not. Dad knew my obsession with selling rocks would wane before they choked his grass. One day they were gone. I didn't mind. I moved on to the next act too.

A Few Clowns Short
of a Circus

Fifteen feet off the ground, the muscular arm of the black walnut tree stretched straight-as-a-compass-needle due west. Both ends of a long loop of scratchy, thick rope, courtesy of Auburn's Columbian Rope Co., were tied around the branch and holding on for dear life. Mine.

A hand-hewn wooden plank notched at each end cradled itself at the bottom of the rope loop. On this and many other summer days, my swing was my best friend and only playmate.

Right after breakfast, I began with a genteel to and fro-ing. By midmorning I was pumping the swing as high as I could, letting go, and jumping off at the zenith of its forward arc. If I do the geometry, at that point I might have been three times my own height off the ground. If you do the geometry, then it's likely to be much less.

I flew through the air with the greatest of ease, thrust my hands forward and bent my two knees. Nine times out of ten, I landed upright and on both feet.

By noon, I removed the wooden seat, grasped the rope as high up as I could reach with both hands, folded myself in half, knees-to-chest, leaned my upper torso way back and pushed my feet skyward for a swinging quasi-handstand. This was all just my warm-up routine for the main performance.

Right after lunch, I reattached the swing's seat and jumped into circus mode. Ta da! I was a famous trapeze artist costumed in shiny, white satin outlined with rows of silver sequins, slippers, and plumed headgear to match. Sitting, I started with the slow and low, to-and-fro. When I reached a crowd-pleasing height, I stood on the wooden seat/trapeze bar, inched both of my feet around 180 degrees so the whole back of me leaned fully against one rope. My left hand held the rope now at the small of my back. My right hand still held the other rope that was now across from me. Then, still swinging high, *sans* net, my two feet told my brain that the board was balanced safely between them and my brain told my hands to let go of the ropes and to extend both arms upward into a graceful and triumphant arc. The audience went wild. Their applause exploded over the countryside startling grazing cows out of their grassy reveries and staggering any crow lucky enough to be passing overhead. Yes, I was a star.

With a slow, methodical reversal, my satin slippers, ever mindful of the tipping point, shuffled me around to where I had started. Next came the dramatic dismount, the balanced landing, and the first of four bows. One in each direction of the compass. I disregarded the crowd's thunderous demand for an encore and went, instead, to reward myself from the secret compartment in the black walnut tree.

Two of the tree's roots met in an arch about three inches above ground-level. Under the arch, squirrels dug out the dirt floor of the secret cave and littered it with nut shells. There was just enough room for my child-sized hand to reach in and extract a hidden roll of Necco Wafers. I pushed past the row of pastels and pulled out a cloudy brown one—root beer—my favorite.

My mother, from inside the house, tapped on the kitchen window to get my attention. She was never in circus mode. Her eyes saw only a grubby little daughter wearing Billy's patched and outgrown "dungarees," the cuffs rolled up from the bottom to just above dirty, grass stained sneakers. Mom shook her long index finger at me three times which I understood to mean, "Don't eat the whole roll of Neccos."

She made a good point. There was no guarantee I'd always be able to find my balance to "wow" my circus audience. On those occasions when I was a little off, the "spectators" graciously allowed me second or third tries. And in between each of those failed attempts, I stopped to take a "balance" pill which looked, ta da, like a Necco Wafer.

Pulling the Wool
Over Our Eyes

*P*uzzled one spring morning by the two empty, fifty-five-gallon steel drums lying on their sides by the barn, Billy and I itched for Dad to come home so we could ask about them.

"Well, when I was a kid . . . ," he began.

That's all we needed. We took the bait, though still dubious that parents had once been kids doing fun stuff.

Within a few days Polly, Billy, and I mastered standing upright, stable, and balanced on the barrels as they lay on their sides. Two days later, we Lawton kids were on a roll. Polly fell off, claimed boredom, and quit for good. Billy and I held daily races. He won the most speed races, but I could keep my balance over longer distances.

As Billy and I were barreling down the yard one fine spring day, Dad came in from the field on his tractor. He jumped down onto the lawn which he liked to keep finely manicured. He wore what impolite company called a shit-eating grin, and gave us, what polite company called a standing ovation. This was unusual and effusive behavior for Dad. I assumed the sight of his extraordinarily talented and well-balanced children overcame him. Little did we know, then, that it was the sharpness of his own double-edged sword that he was applauding.

We thought we were playing. He knew we were working. Like little fools. His regular spring lawn prep included smoothing the bumps that frost, moles, or busy earthworms heaved up. His tool was a heavy lawn roller. Its large cylinder, a tad smaller than a fifty-five-gallon drum, was filled with water for weight. Dad pushed or pulled it with the handle and heavy sweat-producing exertion. It dawned on us in late summer, that not once did the lumbering lawn roller leave its shadowy, spider-webbed corner of the barn. Drat! We'd been had!

Then one day Dad told us about his hoop-rolling days as a kid–rolling a thin metal hoop upright for long distances, running behind it, using a metal rod to guide it. Our caution meters went berserk. We were ready for him this time. We made it clear we would not participate in a mindless activity from the olden days disguised as fun! Rolling hoops, indeed!

Days later, all five of us roared with laughter out on the flat, well-manicured lawn. We took turns with the three colorful plastic items of the newest craze: Hula Hoops. Mom couldn't quite manage the hula move. Try as she might, her wiggles didn't work. Dad had no hips. The lazy hoop took advantage and spiraled to the ground.

Pulling the Wool Over Our Eyes

My siblings and I, with more practice and flexibility, found the hoop's sweet spot and would hula till it wasn't a challenge anymore. Standing in one spot, exercising our midsections, just didn't cut it. "Betcha I can beat ya in a barrel race." And we were off!

Milking It
for All It's Worth

Sometime in the early 1950s, large chain grocery stores began to appear in the city of Auburn. Prior to their arrival, our barn was home to three milking cows and an extended family of barn cats. Chickens were seasonal livestock. In the spring Dad brought home a dozen baby chicks in a cardboard box from the GLF, a farm co-op store. In the fall, when fully grown and plump, the hens were dispatched and housed in the meat freezer compartment we rented from a business on South Street in Auburn. Piglets followed the same program as the chicks.

Farm families learn to work as a team. Often, timing is everything. Mom's innate sense of timing came from her well-established routines. Dad's instinctive sense of timing came after he'd say, "I had a feeling . . ."

My sense of timing was a work in progress.

One of my first chores was to be a go-between at milking time. At just the right moment, Mom would hand me a clean, yellow stoneware bowl in the kitchen and send me out the back door toward the barn. There were times, I admit, that I became fascinated by the lines of the cracked glaze inside the bowl. I stopped walking while my index finger tried to find its way unimpeded through the maze to the bottom of the bowl. I guess I was lagging.

"Kathy!" That was both Mom from the house and Dad from the barn calling me to attention and I hurried on to the barn.

Milking time at neighboring dairy farms was a painfully noisy business with electric milking machines thump-thump-thumping in electric motor rhythm along with the loud whoosh of compressors for suction. Our three cows did not have to put up with that. Instead, Dad sat on a low stool to the side of each cow and back near its business end. His hands and forearms provided the silent energy to milk the cows. Ping, ping, ping, ping was the only sound as the warm milk hit the side of the galvanized steel pail. A green, steel, gravity-fed milk separator stood in the corner near the door accepting each pail full of milk and sending the denser cream down to the bottom where the spigots were located.

My job was to deliver the bowl to Dad when he was almost finished milking the third cow. At that point, the barn cats, with their own innate sense of timing, started one-by-one to appear at their bowl placed on the floor near the milk separator's feet. It was their compensation for being good mousers.

As Dad hung up the milk stool and the cows crunched their hay reward, the barn cats got vocal with impatience. Dad opened the spigot at the bottom of the milk separator filling first my yellow maze of a bowl with heavy cream and then the cats' communal bowl. And then I was on my way again.

With each of my kitchen-bound steps, I watched the silky yellowish cream ripple and roll and threaten the rim. Not a drop to spare because after a couple days we had enough cream to fill the hand-cranked glass butter churn. Yes, kid power was an unlisted ingredient for making butter.

As I turned the crank that turned the wooden paddles, pea-sized yellow cream solids would begin to separate out from the watery buttermilk. Once eternity passed and started up all over again (yes it took that long) the crank became hard to turn as the cream formed big stiff chunks. Then, Mom would place the chunks into the wooden butter bowl and the buttermilk into the fridge. Next, I'd press on the big chunks with the wide, wooden butter spoon and release more water and pour it out. Mom took over the last of the pressing and finally pronounced us "done"!

Our butter traveled, from source to table, about 150 yards with no carbon footprint. And I'm claiming, with no scientific evidence whatsoever, our hand-crank churning offset the methane gas produced by our cows. Thus, zero environmental impact, if you kindly do not challenge my dubious math skills and lack of scientific studies.

Mom, Dad, and I could not be a successful team without the three dependable bovine beauties in the barn. As far as I know, we didn't have names for those three milk cows, but Dad would have known them by their distinct personality traits and milk producing habits. Most farm families know that you shouldn't name livestock that might later show up on your dinner table. Billy staked a proprietary interest in a small, black bull calf that Dad bought. Billy named him Buck. Once Buck reached full size he was dispatched and housed in many forms in our rented meat freezer compartment on South Street, Auburn. One would think there might be some emotional reaction to the roast, steak, or beef patty that appeared on Billy's dinner plate. But no! My guess is that for Billy, Buck might have provided some gender-balancing male bluster for the one boy sandwiched between two inconvenient sisters.

Like a Rabbit
in the Headlights

*I*f we are what we eat, then we Lawtons were the Finger Lakes. This geological region has, as do all others, its own unique mineral fingerprint in its rock and stone. Calcium and its first cousin strontium are two of the minerals that make their way from rock into water and into soil. A region's drinking water as well as food grown and livestock raised there deliver its particular mineral profile into humans.

Tooth enamel is formed in the earliest years of life. A strontium analysis of tooth enamel can roughly determine a person's place of birth. In ribs and other bones, the cells are replaced every five to ten years, hair cells every few months. In those cases, strontium analysis is used for tracking human migration patterns and to help identify human bones or skeletons if there are no other clues.

Since this 1950s batch of Lawtons didn't migrate far beyond Cayuga County's borders, tracking was not an issue. But strontium proved to have powers not subject to scientific proof. First, we had to acquire it.

Our diet matched the 1950s food guide, the Food Pyramid, and most of its items were close by for the picking or the drinking.

Natural springs in the woods at the far west end of our field fed the underground stream that ran through Scipio rock and made its way to our dug well. On its way, it picked up a good supply of calcium, strontium, and other nutrients.

The Food Pyramid of the time stressed grains, cereal, and pasta as the base for a good diet. Scipio fields produced wheat, oats, and rye. Food supply chains were short in the 1950s. Local mills sold to local bakeries and food processors. Only the overflow of grains was transported elsewhere.

Next in importance on the pyramid were fruits and vegetables. For me, this was the shortest link on the supply chain. For a couple weeks in late summer, I lay on my back beneath the red currant bush that grew near the horse chestnut tree, just off the edge of the lawn. By alternating hands, I developed a nonstop system of reaching, picking, and dropping ripe red currants into my open mouth. Mom made red currant jelly each year. But she gave up when the "birds" harvested the currants before she could. Tweet, tweet, tweet.

Cherries and sickle pears could be picked in our yard. Apples grew plentiful on a dozen trees in Tom Marshall's pasture. Tom and Isabell encouraged us to pick them, which we did, under no threat of shotgun fire.

Despite my tainted berry-picking reputation, Isabell requested my help to harvest her strawberry patch. I was asked back each year. Even if my family couldn't forgive and forget, the neighbors trusted me.

Mom and Dad's extensive vegetable garden performed in accordance to the Lawton Standards. It was clean, neat, and well groomed. On time and dependable. Designed to make the best use of space and plant pairings. And when the asparagus went to seed, the garden even had great hair!

Mom and Dad didn't need scarecrows. Any breach of the invisible force field protecting the garden set off silent alarms only parents could hear.

"Damn kids, get out of the garden!" That was Dad for the one-millionth time after a football, basketball, or softball entered the garden's airspace. He knew we weren't the pilfering kind when it came to vegetables. But he knew that footballs and careless kids' feet could ruin some mighty fine tomato plants. Our ball retrieval from the garden reached Mach One speed.

The chart topper from the soundtrack of my childhood would be that oft sung refrain of Dad's, "damn kid." It was not always uplifting music to my ears, but there was no anger in it. The two words were stuffed full of his exasperation when he thought I was careless, used poor judgment, or could do better. If that were the case, he gave a head shake, issued one tsk, followed by a low level, damn kid!

If, instead, I pulled off a long shot, like landing a bigger trout than his, he reworked the phrase. First a broad smile, then the head shake, then a sunny-sounding, damn kid; no tsk attached. But, as in the case of my trout triumph, he'd add, "Well, I'll be damned."

In one way or another, I earned the "damn kid" label so often, it could have been my nickname. But, spoken in annoyance or surprise or anything in between, the way "damn kid" fell from Dad's lips, it felt to me like a term of endearment.

Moving up the Food Pyramid, each category narrowed with the shape of the pyramid. This indicated ingesting smaller amounts than the level below it. Dairy, eggs, and meat were on the third level.

Scipio's mineral fingerprint went crazy on our skeletons with this category. After we sold our own three cows, we purchased from local dairies who purchase from local dairy farmers.

On strawberry picking days, I'd stay for lunch with Tom and Isabell as their special guest. After lunch Isabell and I would go to her hen house to gather eggs for me to take to Mom. I wasn't brave enough to reach under the sitting hen myself. I tried it once, the hen flew off its roost and right into my face. Isabell, therefore, lifted the chicken off the roost a few inches and my hand slipped in to search. The prickly straw nest held the hen's warmth. Warmer still was the smooth oval of the fragile egg that filled my cupped palm. Each found egg was a wonder and a treasure which I placed with reverence into Isabell's wire gathering basket. Isabell chuckled at my delight whenever I found the rare, glittery glass egg she put in a nest to prompt an unproductive hen to lay. Most of the day, the flock free-ranged in their pen, or sometimes flew the coop and free-ranged Isabell's yard.

The strontium-filled waters of the Finger Lakes produced strontium-filled perch and trout. Most found it impossible to decline Dad's open invitation to our dinner table. Our neighbors and our freezer took the overflow. These scaly creatures, cooked to perfection by Mom, added more strontium to our bones.

Sometimes after working a three to eleven shift, Dad went fishing in the dark. One morning, we awoke to find a dozen slick, black and whiskery bullheads, alive, active, and swimming in our bathtub. Dad had been too tired to clean them when he got home.

Billy and I were delighted with our unexpected strontium-bearing guests. Mom was not.

While homegrown beef and chicken were a mainstay of our diet, the occasional Scipio rabbit, pheasant, and wild puffball made the menu. Billy once caught a bunch of strontium-infused frogs. Mom gave a resigned sigh and fried them up. Once.

Dad came home from work one dark night to find a deer munching in the vegetable garden. Minutes before our school bus was due the next morning, Billy, Polly, and I investigated sounds coming from the barn. We found Dad dressing that pilfering deer which hung by a rope from the rafter. Dressing means to remove the blood and guts. Seemed more like undressing to me.

Knowing it was not yet legal deer season, and that kids had loose lips, Dad proclaimed this animal to be a very large rabbit. Polly and Billy understood the truth and the ramifications. I understood it to be a very large rabbit.

The butchering of farm livestock or edible wild animals was a common occurrence in farm country. It was never a pleasant sight, and often brought my tears. But, at the time, it seemed like a common and natural fact of life.

Fats and oils sat at the tip of the pyramid and were the smallest group. Our hickory nuts and hand-churned butter were the local products. As the supply chain lengthened, Crisco, Crisco oil, and oleomargarine made their debut.

We were Lawton locavores. Finger Lakes fine diners. Cayuga County connoisseurs. Our intake of Scipio's strontium no doubt met or exceeded the recommended daily allowance. It explains our strong connection to Scipio, the Finger Lakes, and our solid sense of home. It's bone-deep.

Don't Give a Hoot

The barn emptied of large animals once we started weekly shopping at the Loblaws grocery store in Auburn. Dad's garden tractor and some other small equipment remained. But the rest was my space. Not that I asked.

A sudden summer thunderstorm could trap me in the barn. I didn't dare dash for the house. I feared being struck by lightning. There I was, a little kid in this gigantic soaring space, the barn's tin roof amplifying the pounding rain, and the whole world shaking with rumbling thunder. You'd think all the noise and hubbub would frighten me. But instead, I felt a calm privileged protection. I was alone. I was safe from the storm. I was where I most belonged.

Above the smooth, carved oak stanchions that had once held the milk cows in place, was the hayloft. Its elevated floor went only halfway across the barn. Its open edge was lined up with the feed trough in front of the stanchioned cows below. Hay was tossed over its open edge to land in reach of the hungry cows.

As you know, I taught school in the haymow. My dolls sat facing me at their make-believe desks. My teacher's desk was a weathered barn board laid across two straw bales. Behind me stood the easel-blackboard and chalk I'd got as a Christmas present.

I liked to be the kind of teacher I had in real school; friendly, helpful, and caring. But one day I decided to be Mrs. Romero, Mom's first-grade teacher.

"I hate that woman. I hate her. She was so mean." Mom said that each time we asked her to tell us about Mrs. Romero. Mom had a natural preference to write left-handed. She fell prey to the wide-spread belief, during the 1920s, that left-handedness was a sign of "intimacy with the devil." The cure was to force such sinister children to write right-handed. Thus, they were saved from lives of almost certain criminality.

Each time Mom used her left hand to write, Mrs. Romero struck Mom's left wrist with the sharp edge of a metal ruler. If the ruler was out of reach, a leather strap was always dangling from the teacher's arm. The quick *slap, slap, slap, slap* of the stiff leather left Mom's small hand red and swollen.

Luckily, neither Mom nor my dolls developed any of the common impediments associated with this cure. They did not stutter. They did not become dyslexic. They did not develop poor handwriting. In fact, Mom had a lovely, small, stylish, and flowing script. It was well-suited to her cheerful, often humorous, literary persona. She ate, drank, sewed, and embroidered as a lefty. The fact she had adapted well to right-handed writing makes me wonder if she had been ambidextrous to begin with; a rarity to celebrate. Instead, she suffered in shame and guilt for a natural trait that others believed to be evil.

I didn't last long playing Mrs. Romero. Being cruel to my doll felt the same as being cruel to Mom. It made me sad.

While the barn was empty of large animals, I still had lots of small company. Visiting barn swallows swooped down from the square, hand-hewn beams under the roof in precise arcs. They picked insects out of midair curving back up to hidden nests to feed their young. Mice could be heard scurrying about in the straw pile below. Sunbeams squeezed through a crack next to the window frame and illuminated thousands of bits of chaff and motes that danced in all directions at once in nonstop motion to some ethereal beat.

The principal of my real-life school at Sherwood was Donald M. Gazley (gaze-lee). He arrived at school in Fedora, tweed overcoat, suit and tie. At six feet tall, with thinning hair and dark-rimmed glasses he moved with a relaxed military bearing. Confidence and authority moved with him and he could have been mistaken for the captain of a plane, a ship, or a battalion of the U.S. Army. But instead he hung his suit jacket on the back of his office chair and went forth to captain kids, teachers, and learning through many a school day. While Mr. Gazley was ready to discipline when justified, his quick smile when he passed you in the hall held a hint of a wink.

Two or three times during a school year he would slip, unannounced, into our classroom in the middle of a lesson, walk to the back of the room, lean against the counter, or fold himself into an empty student desk. There were neither words nor eye contact between teacher and principal. The lesson went on uninterrupted.

I guessed it was Principal Gazley's way of springing a pop quiz on my teacher and my class. After ten or fifteen minutes of silent observation, he rose from his perch and slipped out, closing the door behind him with an almost inaudible *click*.

In my pretend school in the haymow, every now and then, I felt a presence. I scanned the dimly lit space until I found it on the rafter next to the window. A barn owl slipped in under the eaves again. His silent, steady gaze was fixed on me and my students. Despite the intrusion, I carried on with the lesson as my real teacher would do.

We must have passed scrutiny because my fine-feathered Mr. Gazley never asked for a follow-up meeting.

A Bum Rap

*I*t's a good thing grown-ups were in charge of summer because with no school year routine, I wandered from one pretend world to the next. Mom kept track of reality. She picked the right moment to announce an event with just enough time for us to clean up but not enough time to get dirty again.

"Today's the Fourth of July, go get dressed for the parade."

Or, "Tonight is Billy's Little League game, eat fast and be ready."

The one I waited for all summer was, "Come in, wash up, we're going to the schoolhouse picnic."

The schoolhouse, known as Sherwood No. 6, stood at the corner of Cork Street and Walters Road. I passed it whenever I walked to Barbie's house. Except for our picnic and a school board inspection each year, the one-room schoolhouse was locked up tight. I don't know who was in charge of the key, but the doors were always open when we arrived on picnic day.

I swear we saw neighbors there we never saw the rest of the year. I was clueless to how news and gossip traveled up and down the dirt roads of Scipio. But the grown-ups seemed right up to date with each other. It wouldn't surprise me if they'd known what I'd eaten for breakfast that morning.

I also wonder how, with cows to milk and crops to get in, everyone in the neighborhood just dropped what they were doing that day. We were all like steel shavings to a horseshoe magnet. No one within five miles of Sherwood No. 6 could resist.

Whole families arrived carrying food and drinks to share. Kids grew busy swinging, sliding, and teetering on the playground. Women young, old, and in between, set the picnic tables. The men made the barbeque fires. Everyone was buzzing and swarming at once.

I liked to throw down the challenge: "Race you inside!"

The herd of small kids ran inside to claim the teacher's desk. Who got there first was soon forgotten as our attention spans became overloaded with contrasts to modern classrooms. Curiosity took over. There was a potbelly stove up front near the blackboard and wall-shelves lined with old wrinkled books. Rows of wooden school desks, the seat of one desk attached to the desk behind it, reminded me of stories of pigtails dipped in the desk's ink wells and *Little House on the Prairie*. It smelled like the museums we visited on field trips. Billy said, "History stinks," but I quite liked the aroma.

I circled the room spinning the big-as-a-kid globe, wrote my initials on the blackboard, tried out desks and decided I liked the last row with no one behind me in case I might grow pigtails. I wandered to the middle of the room to "a relief map." I figured the name came from it being big and heavy, or that the wall it had hung on, or the map itself, became tired and needed some relief. But, whatever! It laid out on a tabletop that took up a big chunk of the classroom floor.

We circled the map table looking at the United States upside down, right side up, or sideways if we wanted. Standing on tiptoes I reached in and ran my fingers up and down the jagged line of Rocky Mountains, dragged my pinkie through the Grand Canyon and traced the blue Mississippi all the way down to the Gulf of Mexico. My fingers' cross-country travel halted when the kid at the teacher's desk rang the hand bell and called for the class to be seated.

We took turns being the teacher and used the books and the blackboard for arithmetic lessons. Our play ended abruptly when we heard the call: "Time to eat!"

Outside, the food table was jam-packed. There were Jell-O salads in jewel tones. A red one studded with suspended fruit chunks, an orange one encasing grated carrots and cabbage, and a green one that most kids steered clear of due to the floating cottage cheese curds. Brains!

Some of the older folks, like Lou and Stell, or Tom and Isabell, brought food I didn't get at any other time, like warm German potato salad and Boston baked beans. Mom brought at least one trendy recipe from the *Good Housekeeping* magazine; that year it was her fruit salad in whipped crème sauce. Hot dogs, hamburgers, and barbequed chicken came hot from the grill. Homemade pickles and preserves drew the *ooohs* and *aahhs*, especially Mom's pickled sickle pears. There was never a better place to sample fresh-made pies, gingerbread with lemon sauce, or Mrs. Van Liew's moist marble cake from scratch, piled high with chocolate frosting. As if this weren't enough, watermelons came out at the same time the outside lights came on to allow us to stay and play a little longer.

That was when Marcia Mains begged me to teeter-totter with her just one more time. Marcia was an occasional playmate belonging to one of the M-families living out-of-alphabetical-order on Mosher Road. Marcia had blue eyes and clouds of curly, blond, bouncy hair and the bubbly nature to match. She was a little bit taller than me, but if we stood face-to-face, I'd be looking at my exact opposite in looks and nature. But that made her a fun playmate.

Built for giants, it seemed, kids our size could barely straddle each end of the teeter-totter when it was held level. We had to stand on our tippy toes. The long wooden plank had no-nonsense metal handles at each end. The board teetered over a rusting, but sturdy, round iron bar which was cemented into the ground.

Our short legs meant we had to take some mighty big push-offs to get the hulking timber moving up and down. Things were going fine until Marcia decided to be a smarty and kept her end of the board on the ground. That left me suspended way up in the air. Minutes went by. It was boring, sitting still way up there with no food and no one to talk to. But from my vantage point, I saw what was happening all over the school yard. I could see Marcia's parents gather their plates and bowls and start walking toward their car. I could see her dad stop halfway there, turn toward the playground and yell Marcia's name.

Being an obedient child, Marcia sprang off the teeter-totter and sprinted toward his voice. My end crashed to the cement and I bounced up and off into the grass. White stars flashed like fireworks, but for my eyes only. Holy Cow! Did my backside hurt! After I stopped crying, my mother made me "take it easy" next to her at the table while she drank coffee and chatted with other adults.

It took Marcia a long time after that and many promises later to convince me to teeter-totter with her ever again. Trust is a must that you can't hurry.

The fateful year came when there was no picnic. There was an auction instead. The school district sold off the one-room schoolhouse and all its belongings. That was the end of our neighborhood picnics. Dad went off unannounced to that Saturday auction. He returned to surprise me with one of the wooden student desks and a separate wooden seat from the last row.

I wonder who bought the United States of America?

Out on a Limb

A map of Scipio dated 1904 labels the open land across the road from the front of our house, *The Orchards*. To us, in the 1950s, it was Tom Marshall's cornfield. What grain-free landscape might have existed on that spot before our arrival in 1946, is left to my fruitful imagination. But the lone Bartlett pear tree, with its desperate grip on the embankment where the field met the road, may have been *The Orchards'* last survivor.

This old, grumpy-looking pear tree conspired with the two strait-laced cherry trees in our front yard to teach me four hard-won life lessons; the first of which I should have learned from Adam and Eve:

Life Lesson One: *Resist temptation!*

Instead, I empathized with Eve at the deepest level. How cruel of God to provide a garden of fruit trees and then to arbitrarily make one off-limits for no other reason than He said so.

As far as the cherry trees went, Mom encouraged us to pick the cherries before the birds did. She pitted and preserved them in glass mason jars for a plump, juicy treat during winter months. Billy and I climbed the trees and picked all that we could reach. Billy specialized in going vertical to the risky top. I went horizontal, edging as far out on a limb as I dared. But that still left about a quarter of the sweet, plump Queen Anne cherries for the birds.

Billy came up with a plan. Standing beneath the cherry tree, he extended the wooden-handled rake skyward and "combed" the remaining cherries off the branches with the rake's sharp, two-inch steel teeth. My job was to scurry around beneath the tree with the basket and pick up the fruits of his labor. What happened next was why child labor was outlawed. Neither of us saw it coming. The lowest point of the rake's arc upon descent coincided, according to the law of Pythagoras, with the geometric center of the top of my head. While cherries rained down around me, three of the rake's steel teeth hit my head with a dull but definite thud. The day went black. Shooting stars exploded like fireworks. As daylight returned seconds later, Billy and I stood face-to-face wearing identical looks of uh-oh. Then it started raining. Blood. Three steel teeth in a row made three-spouting fountains on the top of my head. Billy said the streams were shooting up at least two inches into the air then dripping into my hair, my face, and onto my yellow blouse–the one with the puffy, short sleeves I wasn't supposed to be wearing to play in. Blinded by blood, I let Billy lead me by my hand into the house, through the living room, and into the kitchen where Mom confirmed our fears: yes, indeed, this was a crisis.

The ice-cold washcloth Mom held on my head filled up with blood and soon overflowed. Eventually the pumps shut down and the spouting became an oozing trickle. Crisis stabilized. With Mom applying pressure all the way, she and Billy took me on the trek to Isabell Baker's house for some mending.

We were a one-car, one-driver family then. The car and driver were away at work, trekking was the only option.

Isabell wasn't a doctor or even a nurse. But she was known for her mending skills. The Lawton kids were her occasional patients receiving treatment with the same disinfectants, sutures, and bandages that Isabell used on her regular four-footed patients who lived in her barnyard. Isabell's mending skills included how to calm down a frantic mother during the procedure. Four- or two-footed.

Knowing I would probably fail sometime in the future with resisting temptation, I vowed to adhere to:

Life Lesson Two: Call in the Commissioner of Safety to approve any improvised plans that involve sharp implements.

Back to Bartlett the Grump. On a different day my playmate was Cleo, a year younger than me, skinny and waifish. She lived just a quarter-mile west of our house.

We were pioneers wagon-training it west that day. The tiny yard around the Elf House was our playground. As I scanned the horizon for attacking Indians, I spotted bright green fruit at the top of the pear tree across the road. We left the wagon train to go on without us as the pear tree promised a sweet treat.

Once we climbed the embankment, we found the tree's lowest limbs out of our reach. Climbing it to feast on the pears was not an option. Being girls, we developed a meticulous step-by-step plan by consensus and teamed up to execute each detail.

I think I felt a proprietary interest in the pears since I was the one to spot them. Not only were we playing on Lawton-owned property but also I was older and, therefore, wiser. My rabid taste for sweet fruit may have been one factor, my search for glory, another. All these combined to convince me that I take the role of first fruit-retriever.

I watched Cleo climb the steep slope behind the tree hauling the biggest, sharpest rock she could manage. I picked a likely spot down below in front of the tree where I stood ready to retrieve the pears. Our calculations included Cleo executing a perfectly arched basketball-like shot; a three-pointer, nothing but net. What could go wrong?

She threw like a girl, that's what. The projectile never arched, missed the lowest branch of the tree by a mile. As nothing broke its fall, it dropped, well, like a rock. Its pointed end hit my forehead, split it open, and you guessed it, another gusher. Day turned to night, the stars came out, yadda, yadda. Another trek to Isabell's, again, for stitches.

Had the Commissioner of Safety been around to remind me of the cherry tree incident, I might have switched roles with Cleo. But then I'd regret her being the injured. I felt the tiniest seed of a lesson sprouting inside me. I couldn't put it all together just then, but it had something to do with my own greed.

At the supper table that night, events leading up to my forehead wound were explained to Dad. His response was, a quick shake of his head with lips tightened into his variety of smirk that said, "I can't believe she did that, tsk-tsk," followed by a quiet but audible,

"Damn kid!"

Letting that hang in the air for a minute or two, he followed up with:

"Don't you know those pears need to be yellow when you pick 'em?"

**Life Lesson Number 3. Fruit can be hazard-
ous to your health. Enough said.**

**Life Lesson Number 4. If God were truly a loving God,
He would have tested Eve and me, not with fruit, but with
salted cod-fish gravy, slimy oysters, or puke-y anchovies.**

Putting Socks on a Rooster

$\mathcal{D}$ ad was tall and thin with a manly grace in his movements. He was handsome by any standard and admired for his thick, wavy hair. No one more than Mom admired his thick, wavy hair, even after it turned pure white in his midforties. In fact, her admiration seemed to have crossed over the border into the state of coveting thy husband's head of hair.

Mom was pretty, with fair coloring which included rare gray-blue eyes and straight, wispy-fine, fly-away hair. Mom was fully aware that 1950s glamour was a key part of the 1950s image of success. And curls and waves in one's hair were synonymous with 1950s glamour.

Lawton standards dictated each of us had to have great hair and while Dad's head of hair was the standard, Mom was the standard-bearer. She formed a group of adult female friends and relatives and they gave each other home permanents. Mom's hair, as a result, had bulk, stay-in-place form, curls, and waves.

"Tonette!"

There, I have finally said it aloud. Someday soon, I hope to repeat it, but without the chokehold of terror, without the whole-body shudder, without peeing my pants.

I was blessed or cursed, depending on whom you ask, with pin-straight hair; fine strands, but lots and lots of them. And, straight, or did I already mention that? The Dutch-boy style worked well for me. Simple lines. A bowl, a scissors. That's all it took. I don't know why Mom messed with it. Yes, I probably do.

The Gillette Safety Razor Company convinced Mom (perhaps by holding a sharp object to her throat) that she should apply to my head what its patent application of January 25, 1953 describes as "CHILDREN'S HOME PERMANENT HAIR WAVING KITS CONTAINING HAIR WAVING LOTION."

Children's? I had never considered that boys were victims too.

Waving? Lotion? Sounds gentle, soothing, and benign. But do not be fooled. The advertising cycle starts with the patent application. We kids were doomed.

What category of humans would give the go-ahead for a child's product that required a kid to sit still for hours while an adult, presumably a loving one, executed a multistep reign of terror on said kid's head? I sat in the seat of the folding step stool for which Mom had traded five-and-a-half books of Green Stamps. I was positioned close to and facing the kitchen sink. A stack of towels, a comb, and the evil contents of the Tonette box were within arm's reach on the kitchen counter. It was my job to hand Mom the tissue end papers for each plastic roller.

And so it began.

(Step 1) diagram: Section hair into quadrants according to said instruction sheet folded up in the Tonette box.

(Step 2) diagram: Divide each quadrant further into narrow swaths with tissue-like end papers folded around the end of each swath.

(Step 3) diagram: Roll each hair swath tightly all the way to the roots around a plastic permanent rod.

(Step 4) diagram: Lock the rod in place with a jab-to-the-scalp "snap."

Mom was skilled at making my real head look just like the one drawn in the diagrams. Gillette showed only the back of the diagram-kid's head. If not guilty of false advertising, the no-face diagrams were at least a sin of serious omission. If Gillette had given full disclosure the diagram-kid's face would have had to look like mine and Tonette sales would have plummeted. So tightly wound were the rods that my hairline was an inch higher up and further back on my head than usual. From the new hairline down to my nose I sported a rigid, un-blinkable look of surprise; from the nose down, a grin frozen so wide that "from ear to ear" was not just a metaphor.

(Step 5) diagram: Pour the stinking, rotten lotion into the crappy plastic applicator bottle and squirt each section of hair while it burned the kid's eyes and made the kid cough, and do it fast before the lotion ate a hole in the plastic.

I am only guessing at the words to **Step 5** because *Step 4* had made it impossible to move my eyes or mouth and, therefore, impossible for me to read.

Mom read the next part, the worst part.

(Step 6) diagram: Wait. Wait for an hour.

At least I could get up and walk around for that neverending hour while Tonette was processing me. But everyone, especially the family dog, made quick detours and wide arcs when they saw me approach. Tortured, poisoned, and then shunned. Tell me, what can be deduced about a product that requires:

(Step 7) diagram: Neutralizing

. . . like a rogue spy, an alien invader, or a radioactive accident? The neutralizing lotion was cool, though, and put out the wildfires burning on my scalp. After several whole-head rinses under the faucet, the permanent rods came out at last. Everything from my hairline slid down and back into the place. And, the result? A field of tight corkscrews all over my head.

"Lovely," declared Mom.

For the first two weeks the corkscrews persisted as did the smell of trace chemicals. After that, the permanent wore out fast. Not so "permanent" after all. This did not deter Mom. She pronounced the permanent failure to be my fault for having stubborn hair. Nor did this deter the Gillette Razor company. They came out with new and improved Tonettes. They added a set of paper cut-out dolls to the box to stop the kids from whining for the long wait of Step 6. Finally, they introduced a new and improved Tonette for Stubborn Hair.

That proved my long-held suspicion. Mom was Tonette's secret spy for their Product Development Department. Like most recruited and well-groomed spies, she never confessed.

My savior appeared when I was still nine. Phil, a hair stylist, opened a salon upstairs in a building near the W.T. Grant Co. store in Auburn. Desperate to control my thickening mane with a known resistance to curls, Mom took me to see Phil. After examining my tresses, (straight, remember?) Phil explained to us that what my hair craved was the bulk taken out and some shape put in. And the cut that would do this just happened to be the newest trend, The Boy Cut. He showed us a couple of pictures and we both agreed to it; Mom a little reluctantly, but me, wholeheartedly. I was a tomboy then. Perfect!

When it was done, Phil rubbed something into my hair and told us that I needed to buy this newest of products to keep the Boy Cut looking like the pictures. I took some home with me. It was 1955. Tonette was out. *Grease was the Word.*

Reap What You Sew

"On your mark, get ready, get set . . ."
I took a breath and held it. I scooted to the edge of my seat.
There were my parents up on stage in the bright lights.

Dad's employer sponsored this night of family entertainment.
Before the show we mingled in the spacious lobby with the families of
Dad's coworkers. The sound level rose and the personal space shrunk.
Despite this, Dad seemed relaxed, happy, and proud to introduce us.
Mom was in her social heaven. Polly, Billy, and I were anxious for
the show to start.

While I recognized a few names from Dad's dinner-table stories,
the number of handshaking, back-slapping coworkers that approached
Dad surprised me. I saw him only as my father. Now I saw he entered

this other life each workday. It was a bit wrenching to learn I shared him; we shared him.

The entertainment was a magic act, followed by a sword swallower, then a slapstick comedy act. I'd only seen these kinds of performers on a small TV screen. I was captivated by the bigness and brightness of the in-person show. The distance between me and the life-size performers was so slight, I felt a participant in their acts.

Next, the house lights came up. The Master of Ceremonies wandered into the audience with his mic. He said he needed three couples for the final segment.

"Ladies, raise your hand if you think you have prize-winning skills with a needle and thread."

Mom's hand shot up as did a dozen more.

"Okay, this lady, this lady, and this lady. Follow me and bring your husbands."

Mom, who was the third "this lady," stood up and motioned to Dad to do the same. He hesitated for a defiant moment, then surrendered with a shrug of his shoulders. He was on his way.

The MC directed Mom and the other two ladies to sit on the folding chairs lined up across the stage; each husband to stand behind his own wife. Next, he handed a threaded needle and a four-inch square of red plaid flannel to each woman. Their task, he explained, was for each lady to sew all four sides of the patch onto their husband's pants, while their husband was still in them. The seamstress to finish first would be declared the winner. Needle pricks to backsides would disqualify a couple.

To make things easier for the ladies, he instructed the men to lie across their wife's lap so said patch could be sown to the seat of his pants.

A wave of snickering moved through the audience as each husband took the position which left their rear ends sticking up in the air. They looked silly. This physical comedy obliterated my parents' usual decorum. All three couples looked like overgrown kids enjoying some childish fun.

". . . Go!" said the MC.

Polly and Billy, seated on my right, stood up to cheer. I did too.

It surprised me to see Mom comfortable in the spotlight. She wore her determined and focused face as she stitched, just like at home. Her relaxed body language, what little we could see of it, spelled "I've got this!" Dad's upside-down profile was hard to read, but I think I saw half of a goofy grin.

It was over in a flash when Mom was first to lift both arms into the air in victory. I could breathe again.

Taking pains to inspect Mom's patch to ensure it was sewn on all four sides, the contest judge declared my parents the winners. Their identities were ascertained and then announced. Everyone on stage and in the audience cheered and applauded Mary and Bill Lawton of Scipio; none louder or longer than their children who saw them in a whole new light.

The judge presented Mom the first prize: a shiny, stainless-steel, whistling tea kettle. New on the culinary scene, whistling tea kettles had become a symbol of a modern 1950s lifestyle. It was the first step for the Lawtons into the realm of techno snobbery.

Apart from that stage performance, Dad's need to prove himself was remote and turned inward. A few passionate endeavors ignited his competitive fire; a scuffle between his union and company management; and duels with the regional fish stock. Otherwise, an occasional game of pinochle, poker, or euchre with friends and colleagues satisfied his inner winner-wannabe.

But Mom's competitive edge was razor sharp and honed to a gleaming reflection of her skills, talents, and intense need to win. Was she trying to impress us or set an example? Perhaps she was unsure of herself, struggling beneath the 1950s pressure to excel, succeed, and make a name for herself? Most likely she felt smothered by our needs. More likely, each victory spurred her on toward the person she became as we grew older. She emerged from the 1950s grasping for independence, embracing proactiveness, and molding an identity to suit herself.

But way before any of that could happen, no crossword puzzle landing in her sphere went unsolved. Countless disfigured No.10 envelopes went into the mailbox stuffed with completed contest form with correct skill-testing answer, plus the lumpy, box-top proof of purchase. None of these required contest fees, as Mom's driving ambition was to get something for nothing and the bragging rights and adulation of being a winner. When she won a few mail-in contests, I was happy for her, but the prizes were not sufficient to be noteworthy to a child's memory. Like the token prizes in Cracker Jacks boxes, the excitement is in the challenge to find and reveal them. "The more you eat, the more you want" has been the Cracker Jacks slogan since 1896. The same can be said for winning.

"Pepsi, please," was Mom's voice-recorded entry to the local WAUB radio call-in contest. All she had to do after that was listen all day, every day, until she heard her own voice recording played on air then phone into the station within thirty seconds of its broadcast. Yes, she heard, called, and won!

This time it was another lifestyle gadget; one of the first handheld transistor radios. Our techno snobbery overlooked the thin, tinny sound that came from its static-ridden projections that at the time was a novelty owned by only a few.

From another radio contest, Mom won a free Thanksgiving turkey. The Cayuga County Fair was the venue where Mom lay down her many gauntlets to rival gardeners, pie bakers, and flower arrangers. One year the string bean judging schedule conflicted with the apple pie judging. As the rules required each entrant to be present to answer the judges' questions, Mom entered her yellow and green string beans under my name.

Further rules require the entrant to be the grower, picker, and displayer of the entry item. When Mom determined the optimal bean form and color had been reached, she bent over my shoulder as I earned the title of official picker. Under her supervision, with my utmost care, I washed and dried the beans. Then we rehearsed the display arrangement at home. We didn't discuss how I qualified as the grower, but I was probably on my swing in close proximity on planting day. Guilty by association.

I think the judge may have noted my lack of passion for the contest and any emotional attachment to the yellow and green string beans. But at least I won an honorable mention. That was okay with Mom. Her apple pie earned a blue ribbon.

If she failed to produce award-winning children, well then, she'd just have to be the big winner herself!

Sentimental Journies

I wasn't looking for anything specific when I snooped in Mom and Dad's cedar chest one day. But some fading photographs fell out of a manila envelope. Holy cow! Mom and Dad had once been children! And their mothers dressed them funny.

Further evidence of their former identities fell in my lap on Sunday afternoon drives with no announced destination. We ended up on the north side of Auburn, where Mom pointed to a house and its nearby shed.

"We grew strawberries and potatoes near the shed and ran out in that open field flying kites when we were small. We had chickens and it was our mother (my Grandma Fiduccia) who would snap their necks, clean out the insides, and pluck the feathers."

What? My sweet little Italian Gramma? A chicken strangler?

Or passing through Auburn, "This building was the Auburn Button Factory. It's where I met your father."

Sometimes, the same Sunday would find us in the town of Conquest, a few miles northwest of Auburn, where Dad would say, "Well, the house is gone now, but that's where it stood. The schoolhouse was down the road a bit. Our fields for vegetables up on those hills." Minutes later, "This is Spook Woods. One summer they found a man's body hanging in a tree in there. Older kids dared us to go in, but we never got too far. Too scared to."

If, instead, we'd gone east to the village of Nedrow, Dad told how his mother, that's Gramma Lawton, gave him a sharp stick of a certain length. The Brook Trout he landed with his hook and line he speared onto the stick. When the stick could hold no more of the diminutive fish, Dad knew he'd caught enough brookies for a family supper.

"Then she'd slit 'em open and, use her thumb to push the innards out."

What? My sweet, soft-spoken, willowy gramma? A fish slitter and gutter?

Those two, my parents, had surprises waiting around every corner. What else didn't I know about them? As these new revelations popped up, for a brief moment I'd look at them in wonder. Then I'd revert to seeing what was right in front of me, Mom and Dad.

I spent most of a lifetime with my parents and never learned their whole stories. They had grown up during the Great Depression. They became forward-focused adults who threw meager tidbits of their past out like war-rationed breadcrumbs. They left the faintest of trails to their inner lives.

I wish I'd followed that sparse trail when they were still here. I want to know how Mom's Italian Catholic family reacted to her, the one child of eight, who married a non-Catholic and non-Italian. I want to know the stories of my Fiduccia grandparents from their native Sicily. I want to know how and why they came to America. How did they choose Auburn as a destination? What was daily life like for Grandma who only ever learned a few words of English?

I want to know how Grandpa Lawton's tuberculosis affected his life and my dad's. I want to know how Dad felt when he lost his father to mental illness, to Willard Hospital for the insane, and to sepsis from extraction of infected teeth. I want to know how long Grandma Lawton had been injecting herself daily with insulin. What was she like in her roles of mother, wife, sister, and daughter? What was she like before diabetes made her fragile?

Historical facts I can ferret out. But those aren't enough. What I want are hopes, fears, goals, tears, successes, failures. Knowing ancestors means knowing more about myself. My parents taught me that it's rude to pry. I wish with all my heart I'd been an extremely rude daughter.

Other Sunday excursions found us visiting my Fiduccia grandparents. Mom never taught us to speak Italian nor asked if we wanted to learn. Nor did we ask. The focus of the patriotic 1950s was to be a quintessential modern American. Maybe speaking Italian seemed Old World. Or perhaps it was the one thing of Mom's she didn't have to share with her husband and her children. It was like shorthand, which she learned at business school. It was like a secret code we couldn't break. It was an impervious encryption of her thoughts, feelings, and opinions she shared only with her family of origin.

My Italian grandmother and I communicated with hugs, kisses, smiles, and the delicious language of authentic Sicilian recipes. None written down in ink, but, all written on hearts, big and small, with indelible familial love.

Grandpa Fiduccia spoke enough English to get him by on his job at the carpet factory and to ask his grandchildren if they were being good. I know he understood more English than he spoke.

My "little pitcher has big ears" reputation was well known among my relatives. But my big ears could learn nothing new from listening to Mom, my aunts, and Grandma jabbering away in Italian. When their animated banter reached fever pitch, I'd slip outside to the grape arbor and into the circle made by Dad, my uncles, and Grandpa. Their dialogue, all in English, kept my little pitcher ears busy. Topics jumped around from farming, to factories, to their Cold War worries. Standing in their midst was like standing among my guardian trees. Their strength and protection were palpable.

Mom didn't come looking for me, she knew I wouldn't go far. And since I'd witnessed Grandpa's hidden bottle of homemade apricot brandy make the rounds, the men let me stay in their circle.

If, instead, we were visiting at one of Mom's sister's houses, most of the conversation was in English because Grandma wasn't there. I listened to their recipes, children's remedies, news or gossip about mutual friends, acquaintances, or relatives. When they approached delicate subjects, they switched, midthought, to Italian. Their tone, gestures, and facial expressions told me whether they were angry, worried, outraged, or scandalized. The rest was left to my imagination, which only spoke English.

I sometimes asked Mom later what they were talking about. I always got an answer, but it always felt to me like a filtered half-answer. I didn't press on. I got all I was going to get.

The Devil's in the Details

"Okay, children. Who wants to go for a walk?" asked Aunt Angie. Her sensible black shoes were well suited for Scipio's dirt roads of summer. She rolled up the long sleeves of her black, ankle-length dress with its stiff, white collar signaling the start of our adventure. My cousins and I crowded around, eager to have Aunt Angie's attention all to ourselves.

She was Mom's younger sister. The outside world knew her as Sister Cira Anthony, a nun in the order of the Missionary Sisters of the Holy Trinity. For many years she lived and worked in Alabama and Mississippi serving, as she said, the poorest of the poor. Her tone of voice was calm and steady. Her words were slow and deliberate. Everything she said seemed wrapped in silk and handled with care.

This traditional children's-walk-with-Aunt-Angie capped a day when five of Mom's seven siblings, their spouses, our cousins, plus Grandma and Grandpa enlivened our tranquil homestead with noise and frantic activity. It was a celebration of Aunt Angie. City of Auburn cousins, high on country space and freedom, climbed trees and ran at full speed in the pasture with the same gusto I played hopscotch on their sidewalks. After the picnic dinner, a three-generation softball game broke out with Dad as pitcher, cousin Lillian the lead batter, Billy catching, and Grandpa Fiduccia playing shortstop. Rules flexed, jibes were traded, laughter won the game.

Like a cloud of mosquitos, my cousins and I swarmed Aunt Angie as we began meandering along the neighborhood roads. We answered the questions she asked each of us about our progress in school and our summer activities. She answered our queries about the people she served. "I teach them how to garden, cook, take care of their children. Sometimes," she said, "their lives are so sad that all I can do is listen. And remember, children, sometimes that's enough."

The wandering bunch of us halted each time Aunt Angie stopped to pick a wildflower. She soon had a bouquet for Mom. She'd point to and identify a bird, robins being her favorite. No fire and brimstone; nothing stronger than a honey-coated warning about bad behaviors that might tempt us. Loving nature and loving flawed and tattered humans was her mission and she hoped it would be ours. The afterglow of these walks came from our temporary halos; the holy bounce in our steps, from our fleeting wings.

At family sick beds or funerals, Aunt Angie led the prayers and inspired us to accept death and face the sorrow. When she was unable to attend, we did the best we could with stand-ins, but it never felt as official, comforting, or complete.

It was an event to get a personal letter in the mail from Aunt Angie. They were short one-pagers in her tiny cursive that raced forward like miniature scuttling clouds. Her written voice was the same as her in-person voice. She didn't speak down to children. Her special brand of tenderness peeked out at me from every miniscule space between her tiny written words.

I was baffled when Aunt Angie and Dad teased each other good naturedly like a practiced comedy duo. Their easy and warm rapport didn't square with Mom's labels of saint for Aunt Angie, and heathen stuck on Dad. Aunt Angie was nonjudgmental, focusing on the good qualities she found in people, seeing a spark of the divine in everyone.

Missing in action from all family gatherings and photos was Mom's oldest brother, my Uncle Sammy. A lifelong bachelor, he lived with Grandma and Grandpa. My memory holds him in two locations. The first is at Grandma's kitchen table at lunchtime which was his breakfast time. He slept late.

"Kathy, go say hello to Uncle Sammy," Mom said, as we walked into Grandma's house. I skipped over to the table and stood next to him. "Hi, Uncle Sammy."

In the space of time it took for him to swallow and put down his spoon, I saw him dig down deep inside to find that soft spot. From there he pulled out a sweet "Hi there," a quick but sincere Uncle Sammy smile, and one shiny quarter. He leaned toward me, offering me his smooth-shaven cheek bathed in sweet cologne upon which I planted my kiss. He then went back to his meal and left the house soon after, not one for visiting.

Mom explained that Uncle Sammy, as a soldier, fought in the battle of Anzio during World War Two, and that his bloody war experience left him aloof and a much darker version of his prewar self.

Reva Rollerdrome in Auburn was the second place I saw Uncle Sammy. He and Uncle Al were owners of the Clark Street business for several years. We got to skate for free on Sundays as long as we did a stint in the snack bar or the skate room; Uncle Al's rule. While at the roller rink, the most Uncle Sammy could muster was a barely-there nod in my direction. On an exceptional day, he might add the quick faint shadow of a half-smile.

On Sunday visits to Grandma's house, my cousins, my siblings, and I had the run of the house. One Sunday, Billy, a couple of cousins, and I climbed up into the attic to explore its contents. In the middle of the attic floor stood a large steamer trunk. Unlocked. Well, what's a herd of cousins to do? Once pried open, it took our breaths away. It was packed to the brim with stack upon stack of ivory-colored dice with black eyes and red dice with black dots. Holy snake eyes!

Billy and I, in the car on our way home, blurted out our discovery. Upfront, Mom and Dad exchanged glances. Mom's glance said, "Uh-oh." Dad's said, "I told you so." From their back and forth coded salvos, we learned the dice were Uncle Sammy's and he had a somewhat shady reputation as a gambler. It seemed like Dad wanted to go further, but Mom shushed him.

Later on, in Polly's teens, she was in Auburn's Albee Hotel with her friend and his parents. Uncle Sammy walked in dressed in a long, black topcoat, black fedora, and long, white silk scarf. Three other men, similarly dressed, followed his lead. He started up the open stairway to the rooms above, so he wasn't there for dinner or the musical entertainment at street level. He and his entourage stopped half-way up when he spotted Polly at the table below. He took the cigar from his mouth and gave her a long and chilling look. She understood his unspoken message. "Good thing you're in safe company, now keep your mouth shut." Then he continued his climb.

The Devil's in the Details

Angie and Sammy were two siblings who seemed to be on the opposite ends of the morals, scruples, and ethics scales. Despite this disparity, the words of the American writer, Frederick Buechner, befit them both.

"You can kiss your family and friends goodbye and put miles between you, but at the same time you carry them with you in your heart, your mind, your stomach, because you do not just live in a world but a world lives in you."

Raised in a Barn?

"Sharing, caring, every little thing that we are wearing . . ." That line is from the Irving Berlin song, "Sisters," written for the movie *White Christmas*. The McGuire Sisters sang this song on the television show Arthur Godrey's *Talent Scouts*, the 1950s-version of *American Idol*. The live studio audience selected the show's winner by means of an applause meter, hi-tech for the times. The McGuire Sisters won the show and went on to fame and fortune recording hits like *"Sugar Time"* and *"Sincerely."*

While on stage, Christine, Dorothy, and Phyllis McGuire wore identical, long, sequined gowns, long, white gloves, and used synchronized body movements and hand gestures as part of their polished and glamorous performance. Their smooth harmonies were what success sounded like. And the polished, glittery perfection of the trio was what success looked like.

Barbie and I spent so much time at each other's house and with each other's families that we felt a strong connection to the concept of sisterhood and to this song, "Sisters." We often dressed up in the cast-off, grown-up dresses and high heels we found lying about her attic. We rehearsed our own rendition of "Sisters," complete with charades timed to the lyrics. As we sang the words "I'm going to keep my eye on her . . ." we each mimicked plucking out one of our own eyeballs and placing it on the shoulder of the other.

It should be no surprise, then, that our performing careers peaked in that attic and there they remain, cast off and strewn on the floor with sad abandon. But with this telling, the world has heard of us and the audience laugh-o-meter might register all the way up to CHUCKLE. Thank you, thank you very much!

As for my real sister, Polly, wouldn't you think any teenage girl would be thrilled to share a bedroom with her little sister? No?

So testy was the atmosphere in our room that I came up with the idea for me to relocate my bed and dresser to the haymow in the barn. I moved this plan forward and submitted it to Mom and Dad for their approval.

"She practically lives there anyway," seconded Polly. "Just smell her hair. She stinks. She runs around outside all day, sweats, then goes into that filthy barn. Her greasy hair picks up all the barn dust and God knows what else."

"I stink? I do not!"

"Yes, you do! And I have to smell it last thing at night and first thing in the morning."

So odious was that ongoing ruckus we raised in our shared bedroom that I suspect Mom and Dad's eyes met for a fleeting second as they both gave serious but silent thought to my haymow proposal.

"No," was their jointly delivered verdict that sentenced Polly and me to at least three more years of "caring, sharing, every little thing that we were wearing."

It wasn't child's play–those next three years. Clear lines of demarcation were drawn with mutual declarations they were not to be crossed. Then, they were.

If Polly wanted more shelf space she shoved my chapter books off the bookcase into a pile on the floor. When I'd misplaced my hairbrush, hers found its way to my half of the room.

Borrowing clothes without asking didn't occur for a few more years when our relative sizes were closer. But don't think it didn't happen!

An eye-for-an-eye energy stood upright, weaponized, and ready to strike at any moment through the dense, toxic bedroom air. Neither of us dared inhale too deeply.

I do have to hand it to Polly though. With her vast store of teen ingenuity, she developed a handbook full of evasive maneuvers; one any football coach would find invaluable. Our daily paths didn't cross. Meals and bedtime. That was it.

"Good night, Polly. I don't stink, do I?"

"Worse than ever, now shut up and go to sleep."

I knew she didn't like me one bit. But, somehow, I knew she loved me.

Nuts to You!

Billy assigned me the role of pitcher, or batter, wide receiver, punt kicker, or quarterback depending on what sport was in season. Most of the time I did this willingly, but sometimes, I needed convincing which Billy cheerfully provided. Our practice field was the flat side lawn near the black walnut tree.

In the summer, this tree provided a constant supply of unbreakable, uneatable walnuts encased in a bitter green shell that was leathery on the outside, oily and smelly on the inside. Billy kept a small pile of these ugly nuts at the base of the tree. To this stockpile he added horse chestnuts from the east lawn on the other side of the house.

Horse chestnuts look nothing like horses. They look like Binnol-flails, the spherical Roman weapon with sharp spikes striking out at all angles and suspended from a long chain. All Billy had to do was show up with two or three in his hand, and I'd wisely leave the doll's tea party or my school teaching post and become the sports figure *du jour*.

And Billy had his standards. I was not allowed to throw like a girl. I was not allowed to drop a pass, or overthrow first base. I had to grip the football using the laces and make it spiral just right. Three out of four of my pitches had to be in Billy's strike zone. Any deviation to these standards resulted in Billy chasing me all over the yard throwing horse chestnuts at me. When he ran out of those, the walnuts in their bitter green cover hurt just as much.

As a result, I developed quick reflexes and lifelong instincts about where an object was going to land and how fast I had to move to get to it. Even now, I rarely drop the ball.

Thanks a lot, Billy!

No, really! I appreciate the variety of athletics, team based or solo, that this forced, skill-building reign of terror allowed me to attempt. In our rural school district, athletics were the main source of social activity. Acceptance and popularity were tied to one's athleticism. I wasn't always among the first to be picked for a team, but within the first five. A few times, my peers saw to it I knew the cringeworthy pain of being the last one picked.

We learned square dancing in gym class. Sock hops were held after each boy's home basketball game. Girl's basketball, volleyball, field hockey, softball, cheerleading. I went into each one knowing I was capable of learning the skills to be successful.

Yet, my tumbling skills were pathetic. Something went amiss when I was upside down or head over heels. I managed a sloppy, but passable forward somersault. A balanced tripod? Forget it! A handstand? You're kidding, right? The gym teacher laughed out loud when I did my best version of a backward roll. Coach Billy's efforts would have been useless.

His mentoring, though, continued into our adulthood years. He was my first coach in downhill skiing and golf. The adult sports he took on were individual pursuits rather than team based. He had no further need of me in his own skill development.

His more mature coaching style replaced bruising-by-horse chestnuts with the sting of word-jabs hurled my way. So be it. He's still one of my best friends.

Get Off Your High Horse

O ff the school bus, into the house, change of clothes and off to the pond. Skates tied together and slung over our shoulders, Billy and I towed our American Flyer sleds out to the road and to the top of the hill. A good run for a head start and we flung ourselves onto our sleds. If conditions were right, we could coast all the way to the pond a few hundred feet beyond the bottom of our hill.

Once, an ice storm left the road glassy and we left our sleds home and ice skated down the hill to the pond. Out of control all the way, we were out of our minds and unguarded in the way children dare to be. And, not yet, short on luck.

The pond was neither a natural pond nor a man-made pond. It was the lowest spot in Tom Marshall's pasture just off the road. Heavy autumn rainfall collected there and froze. It was the mirror upon which Billy and I staged a large part of our winter fun.

A half-mile from the pond lived two sisters, Ruthie and Dottie. Overgrown brush and lilac trees filled their front yard. The little you could see of their house from the road, told you it was old and not well kept. In that child's way of knowing, I pegged them to be poorer than we were and not as well cared for.

Dottie was my age and once or twice in the summer might come to my house to play. Ruthie was about five years older than me. She was big-boned and bulky, Dottie much slighter. Ruthie was intellectually slower than other kids her age and often the target of their taunts and teasing. She existed in my world in two spots: on the pond and on the school bus. While most other siblings made it a point to split up as soon as they boarded the bus, Ruthie and Dottie sat together, it being easier on everyone to avoid the obvious—other kids didn't want to sit with them. The rumor was they had cooties. And they smelled.

I couldn't refute the odor, but thinking back, it might have been mostly wood smoke and mustiness from an old house that clung to their clothing.

As for the cooties, in first grade, my whole class was infested with head lice. No telling where they'd originated, it didn't matter. We each suffered through the smelly shampoo and our mother's nit-picking.

By third grade I understood the taunts thrown toward Ruthie and Dottie implied shamefulness. When cooties were mentioned, I not only felt shame on their behalf, but also on my own because of my first-grade infestation. I thought the rumors were mean and I thought they were wrong. But I lacked the courage and the know-how to set other kids straight.

On the pond Ruthie was happy, fun, kind, and protective of Dottie and me because we were smaller. If it had snowed since the last time we'd been there, Ruthie would be there first with broom or shovel clearing the pond. Ruthie didn't have skates. No doubt she had outgrown hers, given them to Dottie, and never received replacements. She didn't complain. She seemed to like cleaning off the pond and sliding in her boots on the ice.

Ruthie planted herself in the middle of the pond, extended one end of the broom to one of us at a time, and became the pivot point around which we flew as she turned. The slick surface tried its darnedest to upend each of us. Instead, it made equals of all of us. On the pond there were no rumors, no taunts, no class or socio-economic disparities. There was Billy, Ruthie, Dottie, and me. Four kids having the time of their lives.

Once school was out for the summer Ruthie and Dottie were out of the picture. They may have gone to stay with relatives, I never knew. But one summer day, Dottie's mother called to ask if Dottie could come to our house to play. We played dolls inside my house for a while and then decided to go outdoors. Something strange seized me at the moment we stepped out the front door and onto the concrete landing. I had been reading the Nancy Drew series. I was both in awe of and resentful of Nancy's wardrobe which was carefully described, as I recall, by words such as fine, wool, sheath, lace collar, silk scarf.

I guess I wanted to get back at Nancy for being socially more sophisticated considering my wardrobe of mostly hand-me-down dresses and Billy's outgrown jeans. I wanted to know what it felt like to be superior like Nancy and here was Dottie, an unsuspecting target.

While we in Scipio had front lawns, Nancy Drew had proper dooryards and I envied her for that. I said something to Dottie along the lines of, "Don't you just love our dooryard?" And, I think I found another couple of ways to use dooryard in the next few minutes thinking it all sounded natural. I think I even remember Dottie's confused look and her statement that it was time for her to go home.

My feeling of superiority lasted only until the next time I picked up Nancy Drew where I'd left off. I was smacked right back into humility and was not happy with myself for targeting Dottie. I think it was the first, and last time, I knowingly and purposely tried to feel better by making someone else feel worse. Perhaps Nancy Drew liked feeling superior. I did not.

At some point, Ruthie and Dottie faded from my childhood. I'm not sure when. Even their abandoned house faded to obscurity and now driving by, most people would never know a house had stood there.

I still feel an admiration for Ruthie's steadfast, patient, and unselfish presence on that pond. And I am humbled. If Dottie remembers the day of the "dooryard" then I am filled with shame.

I have wondered what became of the sisters. I hope they've had kind and gentle lives, but I fear not.

No Cookin' Like
Home Cookin'

~~~

Rich and famous people traveled on airplanes and ocean liners in the 1950s. At least that was my impression from 1950s TV. Both flying and sailing the ocean dangled off the bottom edge of the list of possibilities for Lawtons.

Our neighbors were tied down to their dairy herds and our relatives were hardworking employees and homebodies. Cars, roadways, and highway systems were our bourgeois travel means. We Lawtons never ventured far afield. Why would we?

Each of the picturesque Finger Lakes offered lakeside parks and public beaches. Waterfalls and gorges at the ends of those lakes were free to climb and explore. We had Auburn's Emerson Amusement

Park with merry-go-round and bumper cars, and Onondaga Lake Park near Syracuse. There were summer camps and public campgrounds on each of the lakes.

Eddie's Drive-in restaurant, with uniformed carhops, was located on the west side of Auburn. Yum to its fried-chicken–in-the-basket dinners.

At the foot of Owasco Lake in Auburn, more carhops at Green Shutters took our food orders from Dad's open car window. If it were a Friday, we all ordered fish fries, even non-Catholic Dad, because he liked fish. On any other day I ordered a Coney white hot with mustard and relish.

New York State is littered with regional culinary star-power; Buffalo its chicken wings, Rochester its Zweigle's hots and Nick Tahou's Garbage Plate. In the Syracuse-Auburn area, Hofmann Sausage Company held sway. Its white hot was a slim, white, pork and veal sausage. My favorite menu item, the Coney white hot, was a nod to downstate New York's Coney Island amusement park where Nathan's hot dogs were iconic.

Not only did we eat meals in our car, we watched movies at the two Auburn drive-in theaters. Auburn had two or three indoor theaters as well. We marched ourselves over to every firemen's parade and carnival sprinkled throughout the summer in towns sprinkled throughout the county. The Cayuga County Fair in Auburn and the New York State Fair in nearby Syracuse drew us in each year. Further afield was Fair Haven State Park on Lake Ontario for family reunions. And Oneida Lake State Park on Route 81 North for Dad's company picnics.

We never ran out of places to go and things to see. Even the back-country roads provided entertainment.

"Please, please, please, Dad!" we begged, en route to the village of Cayuga to visit Uncle Charles and Aunt Louise.

If we pleaded long enough and not too loud for his sensitive ears, then Dad would take a detour to the hilarious back road. The back seat was the place to be. The road knew how to tease our childish impatience with its flat start and gentle curves. When we saw the first sharp curve and anticipated the steep dive down the first of three quick hills we begged,

"Go faster, go faster, it's the Whoop-dee-doo road!"

Ups and downs, dips and doodles. As good as any roller coaster.

Any sibling animosity or adult worries were lost with one's stomach on that last steep dip. If the windows were open, giggles and glee spilled out. Someone, maybe Dad, told me giggles were seeds that tumbled to the roadside and grew into buttercups.

Another favorite car ride started with a dusty drive to the west on Mosher Road; inflated, patched inner tubes packed in the trunk. Dressed in our swimsuits, we were on the way to Cayuga Lake. Once Mosher Road crossed Rte. 34B its name changed to Great Gully Road as did its character. It remained a narrow country road, but pavement added a layer of respectability, ushered us along, and amped our anticipation.

Dad drove with Mom in the front passenger seat. I was shoehorned into my usual middle of the backseat between Polly and Billy where I couldn't see anything.

"Help, I can't breathe! I'm going to pass out! I need a window!" That was me causing a ruckus. I picked the right day. All other occupants were too hot and bedraggled by the August weather to raise objections. Polly sat forward and I wiggled behind her and over to the half-open window behind Dad.

I could see the roadside ditches overflowing with tall, deep swaths of Queen Anne's lace. As our car sped by them, those wild filigreed throngs waved and bowed low as if lining a parade route and now, I, too, had been mistaken for royalty. I was a princess riding in a pumpkin coach. The stroke of midnight came two seconds later as Billy pinched my leg. "Mom, he's touching me!"

"Simmer down back there!" we were warned.

As we went along, the farmhouses and their barns popped up willy-nilly on each side of the road. Wide open spaces between them were jam-packed with the scents of deep summer: second or third-cut hay mingled with still-damp swamp grass and the spicy notes of the barnyard mound just topped up with fresh manure. Long, flat, ripening fields of corn and wheat bordered each side of the road.

Further on, farmsteads stood on the north side of the road only, because the rim of the Great Gully was a few yards off the south side, my side. I managed to see over its edge. On one cooler day we stopped and walked to the rim. There was a sheer drop-off covered with trees and brush. No bottom in sight, only the tops of trees. We'd heard stories that wild animals and a lost tribe of Indians inhabited its mysterious and impenetrable depths.

Up to that point, the road took a slow, gentle descent. Then, without warning, the pavement seemed to drop from under us. I held my breath imagining our car would sail off through the air and into Cayuga Lake.

The lake stretched far below us. Long and deep. North and south. Narrow enough to allow a panoramic view of its far side, though the details were thumbnail-size. Fields, orchards, and vineyards sliced the far side of the lakeside into an assortment of irregular shapes. Each piece stitched to the next by a border of trees or hedgerows. It was a patchwork quilt inclined to reach the sky, but not anytime soon. Dust rose in tiny plumes from one of the miniature fields in which a farmer made his rounds. Roads, almost map-size in the distance, zigzagged around the fields. The dark speck of a car in motion might be missed except for the flash of light, a glint of sunshine off its windshield.

While each of the Finger Lakes has its own character, most share this familiar view and dramatic approach. No matter which lake we'd go to, even the far-flung ones, we always felt at home.

Our car didn't fly off into the air. It grasped the steep part of Great Gully Road to its end where it meets Rte. 90 which travels the length of the east side of Cayuga Lake all the way to Ithaca and Cornell University. We turned south toward Aurora. I spotted the sign that tells of the history of Cayuga Castle; the main village of the Cayuga tribe of the Iroquois Six Nations. And just after that, the waterfall and pool that mark the end of the Great Gully. A culvert brings its waters under the roadway and into Cayuga Lake.

An Iroquois legend claimed that the Great Spirit, delighted with this part of creation, bent down to touch the earth, leaving handprints in the form of the Finger Lakes.

My science book claimed that Ice Age glaciers traveled from north to south depositing fertile topsoil here "borrowed" from the Canadian Shield. Earth's eventual warming caused the glaciers to retreat northward, carving out the eleven lake beds which later filled with melt waters.

Both of these claims ring true for me. But legend rings louder.

On the banks of this deepest and longest of the lakes, the ancient Cayuga tribe created apple and peach orchards. Their villages were islands in the midst of corn and squashfields. We knew Dad's corn/hayfield was part of their hunting grounds. Billy and I followed Dad's plow with our eagle eyes fixed on the rich wet earth turned by the plow blade as we searched for more of those black, flinty arrowheads.

As we neared the village of Aurora, an apple orchard stretched uphill long and narrow to the east. The maiden trees, spring plantings too new to bear fruit, were lined up just off the highway like children in a classroom; young ones in need of pruning and shaping. The warm winds and gentle rains that favor the Finger Lakes nurture them and bring them to maturity. Apples, applesauce, pies, cider, Cortlands, Northern Spies, and Johnny Appleseed.

We drove through Aurora, passing the Wells College dock where we often swam. Our choice that day was Payne's Creek Beach because while we kids jumped in to swim and float on our tubes, Dad drove the car right into the lake to wash off the Mosher Road dust.

Once we were cooled off and waterlogged, we packed back into the car and headed for home. We turned east on Sherwood Road and started the steady climb toward the village of Sherwood and then north toward Mosher Road and home.

What I didn't know then was how unique the Finger Lakes region is. And how wrong my naive child's assumption was that life was like this everywhere. I was appalled to learn later in life that most people not only live, but survive, without one lake at their doorstep, let alone eleven or more. Not me!

Holy Glowworm, Batman!

The city of Auburn had more than a half-dozen large Catholic churches most with an attached elementary school. Their curriculum, mostly taught by nuns, included daily instruction in the faith. In contrast, Scipio's Catholic kids attending public school had a half-hour Catechism class following Sunday Mass at one of two small parishes. Then, every other week, we were excused early from our public school classrooms and driven by Catholic parents to nearby St. Bernard's Church for religious instruction.

On these days, Harry Lacey was our frequent driver. Everything about Harry seemed big. Big smile. Big laugh. Big Irish-Catholic-Democratic-Town Superintendent personality smoking a big cigar.

His roomy 1950s car had slippery smooth leather seats. Seat belts were unheard of then. If Harry's big foot was heavy on the gas pedal, we careened around a corner. This sent his daughter, Katie, and I on a tandem back and forth slide from one end of the seat to the other.

Early in our summer break from school, we attended a two-week morning day camp at the same St. Bernard's Church. The first week featured lessons on the lives of various saints followed by pop quizzes. Memorizing rote answers to questions in our catechisms took up much of the second week. At the end of each class antsy kids spilled out onto the lawn to run around while waiting for their drivers.

When the driver was Harry Lacey, well, the ride home was sure to be divinely quick and entertaining.

As the second-week session was winding down, things lightened up. We had absorbed the required concepts of sin and repentance with a sprinkling of guilt and shame. The last day featured a picnic lunch and outdoor games. Then we marched back into church for the grand finale.

Father Hastings held up one of the two Sunday collection baskets, shook it a few times, and told us that in it were folded-up pieces of paper with numbers written on them.

"Take one and pass the basket on to your neighbor," he instructed. "This is a game of chance with some super great prizes."

Wait! I'd never seen nor imagined the collection basket in hands other than those of the duly-appointed ushers. Two of them would stand on each end of a pew, lean forward extending the basket toward the middle. Then they moved on to the next pew. The baskets never left their possession. I believed the baskets, like all the other objects used during Mass were "hands-off" for anyone other than the priest, altar boys, or ushers.

I held my breath as one kid after another passed the basket in my direction. Reaching into it and taking out? No, that was just wrong. Worse yet, for a game of chance. That's gambling. Wasn't the Temple in the Bible story destroyed for just this reason? I could almost smell the black cloud of blasphemy descending o'er us.

Was this a test? Was Father tricking us to see who was pious enough to pass up the game? Or, yikes! Was God?

I watched as the basket moved to within two kids from me. What should I do? What the heck, no one else hesitated. If I was going to hell, we all were. I reached in and pulled out a wadded-up piece of paper. I passed the basket then unwadded the paper; it was number nine.

Father held up a prayer book, drew a number from the second collection basket. The lucky kid showed the priest his matching number and collected the prize. A storybook about some famous saint, a set of rosary beads, a kid's book to follow the Mass. These went to numbers seven, three, and eighteen respectively. I didn't mind because I already had those things. Last, but not least, the priest held up a shiny, white crucifix with a gold Jesus. What seized our weary end-of-camp minds, made us sit on the edge of our pews, and draw in our breaths, was Father's proclamation.

"This is no ordinary crucifix, children. No sirree, Bob! This one glows in the dark."

Tension mounted as Father reached his hand into the basket and stirred the numbers. Around and around and around, slowly. I heard a kid mumble that we'd be there all day. Finally, Father shouted, "number nine."

I couldn't believe it! I'd finally won something everyone else wanted. Mom would be proud of me at last. The crowd of kids applauded my good luck. I walked down the aisle to claim my prize. If this was what winning felt like, I could get used to it.

Glow-in-the-Dark Jesus came home with me and got nailed to the wall above my bed; there to protect me throughout the night.

What was my takeaway that summer from church camp? Not the Ten Commandments and not the Seven Acts of Piety. No sir-ree! I believed I'd been blessed personally by the hand of God with a surefire, go-to lucky number. I liked the way nine felt when I said it. I liked the confidence nine imparted. My future was guaranteed to be lucky.

It all came crashing down about a year later. We found out that glow-in-the-dark watch faces, instrument panels, and yes, Glow-in-the-Dark Jesus's were hazardous to our health. The glow came from radium-infused paint and radium caused cancer.

I dropped nine like a hot potato and picked up eleven. Its luck was untested, but eleven felt more benign. Jesus was taken off my wall and vanished. I'm not sure where He went to, but I can tell you that there was never a glowing nor glorious resurrection in the town of Scipio.

And yet, nearby, in the city of Auburn, other unknown dangers fell at my feet. Nolan's shoe store is where Mom bought my Buster Brown shoes at the start of each school year. Buster Brown, a cartoon character, wore a flying-saucer-shaped hat over his page-boy, blond haircut. He winked with one blue eye shut. Tige, short for Tiger, was his dog's name. Buster appeared to be from Holland. Tige, with his extra-wide, shark-like grin appeared to be a dog from hell. Their tagline was a rhyme:

> That's My Dog Tige,
> He Lives In A Shoe.
> I'm Buster Brown,
> Look For Me in There Too.

But they lied. It was just a picture on a sticker.

A chatty Nolan's salesclerk measured my feet and shoehorned them into the shoes I'd chosen. Then the big reveal! I walked to the middle of the store where the fluoroscope took center stage. It was an X-ray machine encased in a large box the size of an old-fashioned, floor-model radio cabinet. I took two steps up to the platform, feeling superior because I was now a little taller than Mom and the salesclerk. I slid my new shoes into the space cut out for them and looked in the viewfinder. I could see a chemical-green picture of the bones of my feet and the outline of the shoes. Mom and the salesclerk took a peek too. It was proof that the shoe size was right with enough room for my feet to grow.

Sale finalized. I walked out of the store with Mom, Buster and Tige, and a higher level of radiation than was delivered by any Cold War-era enemy, including Glow-In-the-Dark Jesus.

Tuckered Out

*N*ext on my back-to-school shopping list was the Julianna Shop for Children for a new dress or two. Its tagline was "Children looked their best when Julianna dressed."

Mrs. Aronson, the owner of the small specialty shop, was the greeter, fitting-room attendant, and final-sale associate. Mom and I were once-a-year regulars, greeted warmly by Mrs. Aronson with her fashionable New York City accent. While I was trying on dresses, she and Mom conversed about fabrics, styles, and trends. I noticed Mom's speech pattern rose to the occasion and took on a clipped authoritative tone during these conversations.

On one visit, Mrs. Aronson gave her usual greeting as we entered. Right away I noticed a second presence that would make this visit different. At the back of the store, behind the cash register counter, sat the biggest lady I'd ever seen. She filled the entire space between the counter and the back wall. I wondered what chair was large enough to hold her.

Once Mom and I agreed on a dress, Mrs. Aronson led us to the cash register and introduced us to her sister, Sophie, who was visiting from New York City. Despite her enormity, Sophie had a lightness and a radiance about her. Her smooth skin glowed with colorful makeup. Her blonde wavy hair seemed made of shiny silk, and her sparkling jewelry was way above the pay-grade of a sales clerk. Sophie handled the sale process with confidence and ease, all the time carrying on friendly chatter. She studied our faces as we studied hers. She asked what grade I'd be starting that year. I was fascinated by Sophie and didn't want to leave. But the next mother-daughter duo came up behind us to cash out.

As we walked to our parked car, Mom told me that Sophie was Sophie Tucker, a famous singer and entertainer. I now wonder if Mom had known in advance that Sophie would be there. Mom liked to rub elbows with greatness and Sophie sure fit the bill. We saw Sophie on TV a few months later and I felt a glow, this time the rosy and healthy kind, to know I'd seen fame and fortune up close and personal.

Mom would have thanked the heavens and all the saints above for my shyness had she known what I was bursting to tell Sophie the day we met. The message could have been my good deed for the day except it stuck in my throat.

"Just down the street, Miss Sophie," I ached to tell her, "hanging from the ceiling at W. T. Grant's, were ladies' underwear that must have been made just for you."

Let the Fur Fly

*N*uns aren't the only Catholics who have habits. Week after week, each of the Catholic families of our church had the habits of arriving at the same time, in the same order, and parking in the same spot.

Our church, Saint Isaac Jogues Chapel, was in the tiny village of Fleming a few minutes south of Auburn on Route 34. The church's exterior tended toward modern, but the inside had a warm and rustic vibe. A dozen arching, wooden beams soared across its firmament. Polished pews of grainy wood matched the priest's lectern and pedestals holding statues. St. Isaac was a French missionary to the Mohawks in the seventeenth century. The wall behind the altar looked like the stockade wall of a fort from that era. Some twenty upright logs, their tops tapered to a spiked point, stood joined together looking impenetrable. However, each of the spiked ends carried a painted red cross representing the blood of St. Isaac's martyrdom by the Mohawks whom he had tried to convert to Christianity.

On a memorable Sunday, Mom parked in our usual spot, and we entered through the wide double doors, dipped our fingertips into the Holy Water dish. Then we straggled down the aisle like a gaggle of geese with Mom in the lead.

The habit of this multitude that most annoyed me was that families sat in the same pew Sunday after Sunday. Did they fear God might get them mixed up with someone else if they changed seats? I would like to have known if God looked the same from a different angle, but Mom was Mom and so we automatically went to the right side, second pew from the front.

I kneeled like I was supposed to and read prayers from my prayer book.

"Oh, God," I gasped, in my smothered church voice, as I looked up from my prayer book and saw what had just arrived in the pew in front of us. Two tiny, black, glassy eyes, less than three feet away, peering straight at me. Four more eyes had their sights set on Patty Pesek left side, third pew.

Three minks, united in death, now frozen for all time in the act of chasing their own tails. Each jaw clamped shut forever on the next one's backside. They formed a perfect oval that framed the shoulders of Mrs. Rehor, who sat, as always, on the right side, first pew. Why were there only six dangling legs when there should have been twelve? The four forepaws and two hind paws that I could count dangled down in strange places at odd angles that made no sense to me at all. But then I'd never seen haute couture.

These particular animals must have come from New York City along with the sweet Mrs. Rehor and her stylish, but somewhat uppity-sounding NYC accent. Because, as far as I knew, minks didn't live anywhere near Scipio. Our humbler caste of wildlife included squirrels, chipmunks, skunks, woodchucks, dogs, and barn cats. And, usually, we chose not to wear them. Mom had once owned a winter coat with a deep fox fur collar. It lacked any lingering facial features or dangling digits to remind us it had once lived. Therefore, it wasn't a fashion statement as much as a nurturing tool; the softest place for a toddler to lay her weary head for a luxurious nap.

The rigid and rote nature of Sunday Mass double-dared my nomadic brain to soar heavenward or anywhere other than second pew, right side. In Catholic-speak, this is called an Occasion of Sin. Sweet and friendly as she was, I blamed Mrs. Rehor and her minks for leading me astray that Sunday. But, wait! Animals and church can't be mutually exclusive. There was the statue of St. Francis of Assisi right up front by the altar with a bird sitting on his stretched-out hand, a squirrel balanced on his shoulder. Looking up at the saintly face, a reverent raccoon squatted by Francis's foot.

Good thing Billy was not allowed to bring his Red Ryder BB gun to church, or he would have wiped the smile right off St. Francis's face and the bird off his hand. The squirrel would be mincemeat and the raccoon, among all the commotion, would dive under the altar.

My body stayed in unison with the congregation as it stood, then sat, then kneeled, then stood, then sat. But my mind continued its journey. The subject of my drift could turn on a dime. The priest could have said something about a cross to bear; and I'd be off.

My personal crosses jumped in to steer my animal-themed drift. I shared a strange anomaly with the live birds and mammals of Scipio. We each had an invisible red target painted on our backsides which only Billy had the super X-ray vision to detect. Once he had, he took unmerciful aim with his BB gun.

Mom did not object to his shooting at woodchucks. She winced when he shot at squirrels. But she drew the line at his killing birds. Shooting a sister was out of the question. He never asked. He just aimed and pulled the trigger. Mom didn't wait to hear his confession. The penance she laid on him had been quick and stinging. All I'll say is he couldn't sit comfortably while saying his ten Hail Marys.

Billy knew he'd never get a second chance. He milked this ultimate one-time assault for all it was worth. The day after the shooting, we climbed on the school bus and took our seats, me up front, he in the way-back.

"Hey, Raydie!" Billy shouted, even though he and Raydie sat in the same seat.

"I was chasing Kathy down the driveway yesterday. You shoulda seen her legs pumping like crazy on those bike pedals, tryin' to get away. But every time her cheeks came up off that bicycle seat, I'd fire. Bam, bam, bam. Hit her in the ass every time. It was the funniest thing you ever saw!"

"Haw, haw, haw," went all the boys on the bus; those who had a sister, and those who had only dreamed of having one, for just this purpose.

Raydie followed up with a loud story about the time he and Billy carried a live snake dangling over a broom handle into our living room. How it dropped off and slithered across the floor.

"Never saw your mother or sisters move that fast, Billy. And scream! Jeez! Damn funny, that was," said Raydie, who could say "damn" and not get in trouble because he had no sister on the bus.

"Haw, haw, haw."

Then Billy took one last turn, "How about the time Polly was riding down the road and I lassoed her off her bike? You shoulda seen the blood spurt from her knee when she landed. She wailed on and on about how I'd scarred her for the rest of her life."

"Haw, haw, haw."

My face had gone red and my ears burned with anger.

"Someday," I thought, "I'll make him pay for this."

Oh-oh! What about "forgive us our trespasses, as we forgive those . . . ?"

Okay then, someday, I prayed, God, please make him pay for this!

I was learning to expect the unexpected from Billy. I anticipated and thwarted some of his ambushes. But in my deep spiritual examination of my crosses-to-bear, another bully came to mind; came out of nowhere. Well, actually, it came out of the barn a few days ago.

She was a barn cat that we'd had from her kitten days. She was so mewlingly cute and sweet that Polly named her Baby Blue Eyes. She was a family favorite whom we all cooed over; even Mom, whose childhood without pets left her jumpy with ours.

I had just stepped out of the kitchen door and down the back steps in my role as cowgirl. At that same time Baby Blue Eyes ambled out of the barn door caught in her own reverie. My movement caught her attention and she wheeled around to face me. She bolted across the yard at blinding speed coming straight at me. When she got to within four feet of me, she stopped cold and crouched. She began to stalk me, her belly dragging the ground. Those steely blue eyes of hers became entranced in an imaginary big-cat world in which I had been cast as a hyena. Evil intent fueled each muscle, tendon, and sinew that moved her forward. It was as if Billy had deputized Baby Blue Eyes to terrorize me because he had other things to do that day.

Instinctively, I crept backward toward the steps and the door, planning a quick dash indoors to safety. With only a few inches between us, I decided to make my move. Bump! Oh, no. That wasn't the step, it was the back wall of the house. I panicked and jumped. Baby Blue Eyes did too. She landed on my right foot and sunk her teeth into my bare ankle. I yelped; she took off for the barn.

I burst into the kitchen sobbing out my terror. Mom showed some momentary alarm, then scrubbed my wound, applied iodine and a bandage. To my dismay everyone including Baby Blue Eyes went on with their daily lives as if this had been no big deal. Not one human would come to my defense and condemn the cat for its brutality, its mortal sinfulness.

"But she turned on me. Stalked me like jungle prey," I whined.

"You must have done something to provoke her," was their consensus.

And, again, not knowing what else to do in the face of injustice, I raised my right hand in the air, because Catholics don't have Bibles, and I vowed:

1. *For the rest of my life, I will never trust another cat, ever.* (I've kept this vow, religiously)
   The heat of rejection forced me on.

2. *I'll never stick up for any of those traitors who call themselves family, ever.* (Nope! Overruled by Lawton Standard # 6, Family is the first priority.) Sigh.

3. *I will never again put my back to the wall.* (The road to hell is lined with good intentions.)

Amen. And just like that, church was over for another Sunday.

Kathy and her Mom, Auburn, 1951

Fiduccia, Sperduti, Colella, Lawton families. Auburn, 1951

*Edgewater Camp, Owasco Lake   Front row: Marcia Mains, Unknown
Camper, Barbie Van Liew, Kathy   Back Row: Joan Van Liew, Polly,
Judy Van Liew, Billy (standing), Gary Van Liew*

Getting My Goat

The six years between Polly and me meant we moved in opposite daytime hemispheres. By the time she became a teenager, we only rarely met, and then only at the red-hot equator.

"That just galls me."

I'd heard Mom spout that phrase more than once. Knowing nothing of bladders or bile, I did know it meant someone deflated her buoyant balloon of goodwill and left her flat-out bitter. I have Polly to thank for leading me to first-hand knowledge of those words.

Big-deal Polly and her gaggle of teen friends planned an ice-skating party.

"You are not invited," she said. "All you little kids are banned! "

"Oh yeah?" said I.

Running alongside Cork Street between our house and the Van Liew's road was the long narrow swamp that Barbie, her brother Gary, Billy, and I ice skated on all winter long. We sliced evasive paths around uprooted trees, jumped over rotting logs, and broke out our best spins and jumps when we reached the Olympics . . . er, um, I mean the deep, round, open pond at the southern end. Because Polly, Joan, and Judy had more important teen stuff to do, the swamp was usually all ours.

Now, out of the blue, Polly announced she and her gang would hang lanterns throughout the swamp and have a nighttime skating party. Mom not only approved, she offered to provide refreshments featuring her homemade pizza. And everyone else was banned. Oh yeah?

"But, Mom, it's our swamp. We use it every day. How can Polly say I can't go on my own swamp?"

For days and days, my outrage flowed with my tears and I stomped around the house in a fury. "She takes my pens and pencils without asking. She even reads my private diary, and now she's taking my swamp? I hate her!"

A negotiated peace was not reached until the day of the party. Barbie and I could skate during the first hour, the last hour of daylight. And then we had to "beat it," said Polly.

"So then," I said, egged on by my union-negotiating genes, "Barbie and I get our own pizza party too?"

And, that's how it went. The day after the party, the swamp was mine once again.

But there was more. Oh, much, much more that irritated me about Polly. Music, for one. She spent hours in our room with Frank Sinatra warbling from the record player. Did I say anything to her? No! But when Jerry Lee Lewis, or Bill Haley and the Comets played my music, she'd say, "turn that hillbilly crap down, where'd you grow up in a barn?"

"That's not hillbilly, its rock and roll for your information." I'd shout back.

"Well, ring-a-ding-ding!" She snarled.

And on and on and on it went. I've categorized a few below.

POLLY	VS.	KATHY
New York Yankees	vs.	Brooklyn Dodgers
Mickey Mantle	vs.	Duke Snyder
Jazz & Crooners	vs.	Rock and Roll
Girly	vs.	Tomboyish
Indoorsy	vs.	Outdoorsy
Eww! Get that thing away from me!	vs.	Animal lover
Political enthusiast-Democrat	vs.	Yeah, whatever!
Got new stuff	vs.	Got her hand-me-downs
Got away with murder	vs.	She stole my swamp!

"Brother, Can You Spare a Dime?"

~~~

Shirley Temple movie was sure to bring it on. As the end credits rolled down the TV screen, Polly, Billy, and I hunched our shoulders against Mom's predictable lament:

"Why couldn't just one of my children be blonde-haired, blue-eyed, and talented?"

A moment followed during which each of us had the chance to think of an answer. But we were dumbstruck. Polly and Billy shrugged off the question as they unhunched their shoulders and resumed their cool lives. They were old enough to sense that Mom's question may have been rhetorical. Whereas, I believed each question had a logical answer and each wrong could be righted.

I vowed to become that famous kid in whose glow Mom deserved to bask. Granted, off the mark I had certain handicaps, namely dark brown hair and darker brown eyes. My stage talents had never been tested. But didn't willpower alone win races and get puffer-bellies up steep inclines? I prepared myself to become a child prodigy, a Whiz Kid, or a Mouseketeer. Like the Little Engine That Could: I think I can. I think I can. I think I can.

You may, then, have heard about my 1953 stage debut at the extraordinary age of eight. I had been cast as one of the dimes in the March of Dimes school assembly. There was a dollar's worth of us parading on the gymnasium stage that day. We were each costumed in a three-foot high cardboard circle with a hole cut in its middle to show our face. The frame of this 3-D dime sat on our shoulders and we balanced it with both hands. So thoroughly had the cardboard and our bodies been tin-foiled that we should have been picking up short-wave radio programs. Now lest you find mirth in those newly minted coins, let me impress upon you how serious our message was that day.

Polio had become a global epidemic. Not even President Roosevelt had escaped it. Except for Black Bart (alias, Billy) I'd never had a real enemy. But polio terrified me. I tried to see myself in those posters as one of the little girls in frilly dresses, the hems of which grazed the cruel, industrial metal leg-braces. Bent crookedly over their crutches, they were about to swing their heavy legs forward in order to "walk." I would have been a miserable victim; not smiling like the kids in the posters. I imagined myself locked in an iron lung letting it breathe for me—no thanks! Someone died in one when the power failed. How could I still be me, I wondered, if I could not run, not bike, not hide-n-seek, not escape the wrath of Black Bart?

It became my job, the Ninth Dime, to step forward from the straight row of dimes, deliver the play's key line of dialogue, and then step back with the rest. As the Eighth Dime on my right finished his line of dialogue, I counted to three and stepped into the spotlight. I stood silent for a second or two longer than we had rehearsed which if I had been the calculating type would have upped the drama. But I was the panicked type whose brain and mouth went out of sync up on stage. I was the type whose hands sweated and words trembled. But I took a deep breath and in the loudest, clearest theatrical voice I could muster, I yelled my one line.

"Take home a March of Dimes card today!"

This card I had shouted about was made of heavy-duty paper with several lines of slots into which single dimes would fit perfectly and stay in place. All school children went out collecting dimes from family and neighbors and brought the filled cards back to school so polio could be defeated. Damn right we filled them. We were scared. The polio virus lurked in public swimming areas, so we couldn't go anymore. Panicked parents speculated about where else it lurked and we couldn't go there either.

But, back to my performance . . .

Paralysis held me in the spotlight long enough to let my message travel to the back of the audience and to give the first pair of hands time to clap. I imagined they would belong to my mother. And they would have, except the Tenth Dime to my left tripped when stepping forward and almost lost his coinage. The laughter that ensued drowned out any would-be ovation for me. At the end Mom told me I had done "fine" which I knew in my heart didn't mean star-quality. It meant mediocre. It meant small change.

My next chance to be somebody came the next year, 1954. I became a Polio Pioneer; one of 1.8 million third-graders taking part in the clinical trial of Salk polio vaccine. We wore Polio Pioneer buttons proudly and parents kept safe our wallet-size ID cards. Over a five-week period, we showed up three times in the nurse's office at school for a shot. We formed two long lines. One line received the Salk vaccine, the other got a placebo. Who-got-what was kept secret from us. There was a third group who didn't show up at all; the control group. It didn't seem fair they, too, were Polio Pioneers. A pin and card for doing nothing? But helping to make history, I reminded myself, could make Mom proud of me, especially if I were a Pioneer who had received the real vaccine.

A year later, the bitter truth arrived in a letter. My line had been the placebo line. Worse yet, I had to roll up my sleeve three times more to get the real thing. It was then that my attitude took a turn on the proverbial dime. I felt I had enough on my plate just being a regular kid, without trying to be a famous one. Mom, however, never gave up hoping or lamenting.

And I never gave up feeling not quite good enough.

About this same time, another cardboard coin card showed up in my life. This time the slots were much bigger and the church wanted us to fill the card with a quarter for each day of Lent. Lent had a lot of pesky rules to it and I didn't like the guilt attached to the piece of candy that I ate by mistake after I had "given it up." But Lent didn't terrify me like polio. Filling up the March of Dimes cards had felt like a valiant effort from everyone on the planet to defeat a common enemy. If filling up Lenten cards had meant wiping out Lent, then I would have been a begging fool to fill those quarter slots.

Was it so bad to remain a mere two-bit player and never the star? Meh, things could be worse.

A Little Off-Kilter

*B*efore TV, when radio was our main entertainment, we had to imagine not only what the characters looked like based on their voices, but also to figure out the settings. I wouldn't have known what an old-time western saloon looked like, but I knew the sound of the squeaky hinges of the swinging doors prefaced by music portending danger when the Lone Ranger, who abstained from smoke and drink, entered to confront the villain. And, I somehow knew to imagine the dust kicked up by the fake sound of the galloping horse hooves.

With TV, less was left to my imagination, but more was open to my discernment. Not only could I see how I stacked up next to Shirley Temple, but also how the Lawtons of Scipio stacked up next to TV families. In comparison, our rusty hinges squeaked loudly.

Series such as *I Love Lucy* and *Father Knows Best* had focused storylines with obvious lessons even a little kid like me could spot. Other entertainment forms offered subliminal messages that by-passed my active brain, but stuck to my subconscious.

The Ed Sullivan Show was a Sunday evening variety show and a staple at our house. Ed, a former-journalist-turned-TV-host, spoke in a flat, newsreel voice and had a face, as they say, made for radio. Expressionless. His guest comedians scored instant laughs by exploiting the lack of Ed's smile-musculature.

We all took our favorite TV viewing spots in the living room. Mom sat on one end of the sofa with knitting in her lap, the yarn unspooling from a bag on the floor, the needles clacking their soft rhythm. Polly claimed the sofa's opposite end. A teen magazine open on her lap, was to thwart boredom as most of the acts fell short of her sophisticated teen taste. I knew she was only there for the scheduled crooner. She'd then be able to gush about him with her classmates on Monday. Dad lounged in his dark green recliner after tapping out his pipe in the ashtray. Billy and I plunked down, cross-legged, on the floor close to the TV.

Ed introduced Eric Brenn as an act to amaze and entertain us. Eric stood behind a twelve-foot table with four thin, flexible sticks anchored upright and equidistant along its length. He spun one clear glass bowl atop a stick and wiggled the stick to create a strong momentum: the same with bowls two, three, and four. Then, one at a time, on the table's surface, in between the sticks with spinning glass bowls, he set six white dinner plates whirling on their edges.

By then, the first bowl's momentum slowed to a dangerous wobble. With a faux look of horror, and a practiced stumble, Eric reached the flailing bowl, wiggled the stick, set the bowl spinning to avoid disaster. On and on this went, with near mishaps Eric pretends not to notice till the last second. We inhaled as the tension mounted. At last all bowls and plates were spinning in good health. To further test our endurance, he added the ridiculous—he flipped a tray holding twelve glass tumblers and twelve teaspoons. In that one flip, each spoon jumped into its intended tumbler. The pressure of it all kept us on the virtual edge of our seats and laughing.

Finally, Eric went down the line, stopped and stacked each spinning plate, tossed each glass bowl into the air with a flick of the stick, and caught each one. With all props still and safe, we breathed easy. The audience applauded loudly and the show went to a commercial break.

Eric Brenn leaves no doubt that staying in balance requires just the right amount of momentum, a watchful eye, and good timing. It would be one of those things my kid brain and body intelligence soaked up, filed away, and transformed to a hidden awareness. The beauty is, in the moment of need, it responds in a silent instant, keeping me on my feet.

Author's note: *I've been forced to calculate the number of calories I burned while writing the six preceding paragraphs about Eric Brenn. To save time and because I'm seriously allergic to advanced algebraic equations, let's just all agree it was one hundred calories, shall we?*

Albert Einstein gets the blame for this embarrassment. While he agreed wholeheartedly with my Eric Brenn premise, Albert was not focused on expending calories. In one slender sentence, the svelte Mr. Einstein wrote, and I quote:

"Life is like riding a bicycle, to keep your balance, you must keep moving."

Genius!

Live entertainment had an even more visceral effect on me than TV viewing. I learned this sitting in a pitch-black auditorium, while a beam from a distant wall sconce bounced off my parents' eyeglasses allowing me to see their shadowed features.

Up on stage in the spotlight, a magician placed his gleaming saw blade into the top of the wooden box that imprisoned his female assistant. Minutes before, she stood beside the box with a wide smile and a brief, but sparkly costume. Now, I saw only her curly blond head at one end and silver high-heeled shoes at the other. She no longer smiled. The sawing began. The audience, including me, gasped as the saw blade presumably ripped through skin and bone.

Sitting in the dark erased me. The real me felt like I was on the stage being sawed in half. Empathy, again. I looked at Mom. Her face wore a knowing, unworried half-smile. Dad's face, relaxed, held his slight grin. I trusted, then, that the magic act was a trick, an illusion, not a real bloodbath. But I didn't relax until the woman jumped from the box whole and unbloodied.

My own mind tricked me with an illusion of its own. I believed the status quo was permanent. There would always be a rabbit in the top hat. Rules would always be followed. My parents would always stay together. They would always keep me safe. I would remain in the audience trying to believe, not up on stage in the spotlight.

Our family was progressing in life with enough oomph to keep us spinning and on our sharp edge. But one day, the plot began to thicken. Our momentum stalled, and the Lawtons of Scipio developed a precarious wobble.

My status quo began its downhill slide toward wrecked illusions in 1953 with the Barry brothers. I was seven years old.

Life and Limb

*M*om and I were dressed in our Sunday clothes even though it was Saturday. Since it was just the two of us, I got to sit in the front seat while she drove us down Bluefield Road. I'd never seen a blue field around here, but there must have been one once, otherwise why would they have picked that name?

But anyway, Mom told me that something bad had happened to the Barry brothers and we needed to visit their family to make them feel better. A tractor-trailer knocked Bernie and John off their bikes as they road on South Street near Auburn. John was in the hospital. And Bernie was dead.

Last Sunday, Bernie sat in the church pew in front of me for our Catechism class. Bernie and John are both a little older than me, but I'd outgrown the younger class and moved up. I only knew

Bernie and John from church on Sunday and our church picnics, but I liked them.

That Sunday, Father Hourihan told us the story of the Irish saint, Saint Brendan, for whom Father had been named. Father's plain, brown, floor-length vestments and his deep voice wrapped in lilting brogue had me thinking Saint Brendan stood right in front of us.

My sight line to Father's face slipped just a little and I noticed what I thought was a scar on the back of Bernie's head. It looked like the outline of New York State except Long Island was missing. Now, I'd never have the chance to ask him how it happened.

I sort of knew what dead was. Mom and Dad went to the funeral parlor when someone they knew grew old, sick, and then died. They were solemn while getting ready to go and quiet when they come home. People on TV died and were shown in a coffin in a funeral parlor; or their coffin was shown being lowered into the ground. I'd seen scary movies about dead people waking up. And I'd seen a dead cat in the barn once. But death had kept its respectful distance from me.

As soon as Mom and I went through the Barry's side door and into the kitchen, I smelled the strongest perfume in the world. It was awful sweet and hurt my nose. Mom hugged Mrs. Barry and Mrs. Barry said, "Bernie is in the living room, go right in."

I didn't feel well all of a sudden. This wasn't a funeral parlor. Should Bernie be there? Mom pulled on my hand to get me started toward the living room. The air was thick with hush and quiet. Mom just nodded her head to the people we passed in the dining room on our way to the living room.

Framed by the arched doorway of the living room, a wooden coffin sat up on a table surrounded by tall bunches of flowers. More flowers filled the corners of the room. I saw the side of Bernie's head and face. Mom led me up to the kneeler right in front of the coffin.

She whispered to me to kneel and say a prayer for Bernie and one for John, still in the hospital. But for some reason, I couldn't think of any of my prayers. I felt woozy and thought I should say a prayer for myself. But I wanted to know what "dead" looked like. I made myself look at Bernie.

He looked like he was sleeping, but I knew it was more serious than that. No eyelashes blinking, no breathing in and out. I knew he would never wake up again, never ride his bike again, and never sit in front of me at church again.

I remembered the words to *Our Father* and moved my lips to the words I didn't say out loud. Bernie's black horned-rimmed glasses were folded shut in the pocket of his Sunday church suit. The corner of his mouth looked like it wanted to smile but his lips looked frozen. I saw Bernie only from the waist up because the rest of him was covered in a white, silky blanket that seemed too fancy for a boy. I wondered if that's what Bernie thought too. But maybe when you are dead, you don't notice stuff like that.

Mom and I stood up from the kneeler and she led me to a chair right next to Bernie's coffin. I sat down. She handed me a rosary. Mrs. Barry, Mom, and other ladies from the Altar Society knelt all around the living room floor facing Bernie and started saying the Rosary.

"Hail Mary, full of grace . . ."

Their chanting made me drift off into thinking about Bernie's scar and I wondered why God bothered to give him a scar if he was going to kill him anyway. Maybe the scar had been a warning and Bernie didn't listen, so God killed him. But, why then were we praying to God? Confused, I thought for the time being, I'd just do as I was told and figure it all out later.

". . . pray for us sinners, now and at the hour of our death. Amen."

Then, Mr. Barry arrived home from the hospital and all the adults moved into the adjoining dining room. They asked about John's broken leg. I was the only kid except for Bernie. I was alone in the living room in my chair, frightened by Bernie because he wasn't really Bernie, and afraid to move. I wondered if at night they closed the trap door to the casket just in case (my imagination kicked in) Bernie came back to life and wanted to walk around the house. I wondered how it would feel for Bernie when that door is slammed shut for good, and he and the coffin are covered with dirt. I thought, it will be cold and dark, and frighteningly alone.

I was glad when Mom said we had to leave. I took one more look at Bernie because I could not understand how a kid who wasn't old or sick can be alive one minute and dead the next. Could I die too?

I didn't like the bulky, black, and shapeless fear that settled in my stomach. But neither did I know what to do about it.

A New Leaf

*J*ust about this same time, Mom had a surprise for us. She was going to have a baby. It was growing in her stomach. Another Lawton. I'd never imagined that.

Chances are with Mom, then forty, and Dad forty-six, they hadn't imagined it either. But, wow, now I could be a big sister and never have to endure the "baby of the family" label again. It would be a living doll that I'd play with. This was exciting.

That summer, Mom started knitting booties and a sweater. A hand-me-down crib arrived from one of our relatives. Day-to-day life stayed the same, as the baby wasn't due until after Christmas. As Mom's belly expanded, I laid my head on it to listen to all the gurgling sounds and feel the baby kick my cheek or ear. A girl or a boy? The suspense meter inched upward.

Against the Grain

Knee high by the Fourth of July is the patriotic good omen for growing corn. It proved true for Scipio farmers who gambled on corn crops in 1953. That year, during the summer I turned eight, the hard-packed dirt roads of Scipio were the only bodies of soil for miles around that resisted the urge to become cornfields. The north side of Mosher Road was lined with corn crops belonging to Tom Marshall and Burton Minde. Dad's cornfield lay on the south side of the road. Our house and yard became a tiny island in a cornstalk sea. By mid-August, the tide came in, the tassels came out, and we lost sight of the entire neighborhood.

Despite our parents' warning not to, Billy and I with various playmates (unnamed to protect the guilty) sneaked across the road and into Tom Marshall's cornfield. The rows ran east and west, parallel to the road. The towering cornstalks were packed tight into each row like defensive linemen on their own five-yard line. Therefore, if only two rows separated me from my partners in crime, we were blind to each another. A game of hide-and-seek could last all afternoon. We raced up and down the narrow spaces between the rows despite the razor-sharp leaves slashing our arms, cheeks, necks, and knees. Strangely, I don't remember ever having to explain the red, scabby evidence of our misconduct.

Running north and south against the grain, was akin to crashing head-on through the impenetrable Buffalo Bills defensive line. The cornstalks tackled us at the ankles and turned us each into Clem Kadiddlehopper (a Red Skelton character). We fell face-first and drunk with laughter into the dirt. Anything that amused us was worth repeating. For hours if necessary.

Cleo, of the pear tree fiasco, was my playmate for this day. Her mom, just that morning, cut Cleo's straight, brown hair. With short-chopped bangs and straight-cut ends all around, she looked like Buster Brown's twin sister minus his silly hat. Cleo's house was about a quarter mile west of our house, but invisible due to the surrounding cornstalks.

The two of us spent hours one morning running the rows of Tom Marshall's cornfield. Her dad was Tom's hired hand. That, we reasoned, gave us permission and protection. Then for a change of pace, I got Mom's permission to walk to Cleo's house. It seemed odd to me, a blue panel truck parked on the wrong side of the road next to our cornfield, facing west, halfway between Cleo's house and mine. It didn't belong to anybody in our neighborhood.

When we came even with the truck, a man leaped from the driver's side. He walked around the front of the truck and held out two pieces of candy as he asked our names. While we unwrapped the candies, he squatted down between us, talking nonstop, and pulled me onto his knee. His finger went inside the leg of my summer shorts, inside my underpants and touched me, there. I wriggled off his knee and out of his grasp. It was only the briefest of moments. But it was enough.

"Come on Cleo, let's go," I said, seeing that he was reaching for her. We walked away. He climbed back in his truck, turned it around in the road and went the opposite way.

Cleo said, "He was real nice."

But I said, "No, he wasn't, he touched me under my shorts." We reached Cleo's yard and I took refuge in our imagined world of Cowboys and Indians. I never mentioned that day to anyone because I knew there was something wrong and it might be me.

September came, and with it a new beginning. The third-grade classroom into which my teacher Mrs. Haines welcomed me was neat and polished. The janitors had lined up our desks with precision and wiped the blackboards clean of all the chalk dust from last year's class. The floors were gleaming and slippery. We ran and then slid on them with our new shoes.

I loved the smooth shine of the brand-new, yellow No. 2 pencils, the waxy smell of the untouched sixteen Crayolas, and the used but brand-new-to-me third-grade reader thick and heavy with the mystery of new words and stories. I lifted the top of my school desk and arranged my supplies neatly. Everything in front of me sparkled with potential.

After school we made the most of what hours of daylight and summer weather were left. One afternoon, the bus dropped us off at home, I changed out of my school clothes, and with Mom's okay, rode my scooter to Cleo's house to play for an hour. When Cleo's mother told me the hour was up, I picked up my red scooter from the edge of the lawn and started for home. As usual, I balanced on my right leg and pushed with my left along the dirt and gravel surface toward home.

Halfway there, that same blue panel truck came down the road toward me, pulled over to the wrong side again and parked. As I neared it, the same man was leaning back against the truck's passenger-side's front fender looking casual and relaxed with one foot crossed over the other. He'd left the driver's side door open like the last time, but this time the passenger's side door was wide open too. He and the truck were just a few feet away from me.

"Hi Kathy," he said, as he stepped toward me and held out an opened full bag of Oreo cookies and invited me to take one.

Something like a shiver ran from my toes up to my head. Unlike a shiver, it didn't go away, and it made my ears and my whole head feel hot like I might explode. It was hard to breathe, but I didn't stop.

"No thanks, it will spoil my supper." The words just came out without me thinking and all the time my left foot kept me and the scooter moving forward at the same nonchalant pace. Just act normal until you're out of his reach, I thought.

Once I moved past his truck, I threw my scooter into the ditch and ran as fast as I could toward home. I didn't know if he was running after me which made me run even faster. As I ran, I realized why he parked where he did. I could see our house's chimney top, but when I looked for our kitchen window, where Mom often stood, all I could see was corn. And that meant my mother couldn't see me.

The second my shoe crossed the fine line between dirt road and our lawn, I was home. I was safe. He couldn't get me. But adrenaline and terror propelled me at superhuman speed, it seemed, to our front door.

I ran screaming into the house yelling about a man who had scared me. I told Mom about what had happened the other time. The rest is shadowy, but Mom called Dad from wherever he was. They threw me down on the couch, pulled down my underpants and looked to see if anything was wrong. I wondered what could be wrong, but they didn't say, and I didn't ask. Being safe in my house and with my parents was all I cared about.

The next day, it must have been a Saturday, a sheriff's car came to our house. Mom and Dad called me indoors to talk to the deputy. He told me they had been trying to catch the man in the blue truck because "he's not a good man and bothered other children." The deputy asked me lots of questions about both times I'd seen the man and I had to point between my legs to show him where the man had touched me.

A few days later this same deputy came back with a second one and they had Cleo with them. Mom and the deputies told Cleo and me that we were to play at the edge of the road just out of sight of our house. The deputies were going to hide in the cornfield behind us. If the man came along and stopped to talk to us, they would rush out and arrest him.

As we walked to our positions, I looked back at Mom. She had taken up the role of a casual lady in a lawn chair enjoying the fresh air and knitting booties with blue yarn spooling out of a bag at her feet. I felt better knowing she was close by, though to me, it looked unnatural to see her knitting outdoors.

We spent most of one day and half of a second one playing alongside the road, but the man never showed up.

A few weeks later, Polly, Billy, and I lined up in just that order to get off the school bus as it slowed down to stop at our driveway. Billy said, "Wow, look at that, there's a police car in our driveway." All the kids on the bus moved to the windows for a look. They saw what I saw; a uniformed deputy standing outside his car talking with both Mom and Dad. Dad was usually at work when we got home from school. Something big was going on. As we walked up the driveway, the deputy opened the back door of the police car and pulled a guy in handcuffs out of the car.

"Kathy," said the deputy, "is this the man you told us about?"

"Yes," I said.

"Tell the little girl that you are sorry," the deputy said to the guy in handcuffs.

"I'm sorry," he said, but he was looking at the ground, not at me, and I could tell he didn't mean it.

The deputy put the man back in the car and drove away. We went into the house. Dad said the police had arrested the man and were taking him to jail. I thought everything was going to be okay.

The next morning when we climbed back on the school bus, and before we got to our seats, Billy called loudly to his buddies in the back, "Hey, guess what? We had some guy arrested for bothering my sister." Sheriff Billy had no more idea what the cops and our parents had meant by "bothered," than I would have had, before all this started.

But with all eyes on me, I was quick to sit down. As the bus continued down our hill, I shrunk, faded, and hid somewhere inside myself blanketed with a feeling I didn't then know how to name. It was shame. Unearned shame, but I wouldn't know that for a long, long time. Trauma and fear with no outlet or resolution crowded into each cell of my body.

Some months later, I rode along in the car with Dad as he headed to nearby Union Springs to go to the bank and post office. I waited in the car for him as usual. I watched him walk in front of our car to get to the sidewalk. I froze. Across the street I saw the blue truck that the man drove, parked and empty at the curb.

He wasn't in jail anymore! He could be anywhere. I locked the doors.

Terror started at my toes, again, and reached my ears in record time. The passing seconds pounded inside my head. As soon as Dad came out of the bank's door, I unlocked the doors. If Dad saw the truck, he gave no clue.

I didn't tell Dad that I'd seen the truck or about my panic. I just pretended to be calm and cool. Mom and Dad were enraged with this man and what he did. I didn't want them to be upset all over again. No one talked to me after the day of the arrest, nor I to them, about the man or what happened.

It was the 1950s. Hush, hush. I was expected to forget the whole thing. And Mom and Dad didn't know the right words.

The feeling of terror that propelled me away from the clutches of a pedophile became a constant and unwelcome companion. Whenever I was alone it lurked just under my skin, ready to pounce at any real or imagined threat. It rode on top of my skin when I walked or bicycled alone which was just about everywhere I needed to go. Mom sensed my fear at first because she would tell Billy to walk with me if I was going to Barbie's house. Of course, "with me" to Billy meant he walked down on the edge of the swamp where I couldn't see him while I was up on the road. And he'd taunt me with 'little baby's afraid' as he jumped out way ahead of me or suddenly from behind. He annoyed me as usual, but I knew I could count on him if I needed him.

When I allowed myself to think about the Oreo cookie day, which wasn't often, I pictured the truck with its passenger-side door wide open. That made it easy for him to have thrown me into the truck and locked that door behind me. He must have figured he could get around to the driver's side before I could escape from the driver's door. That means he planned this whole thing, in detail. That also means he was the hunter and I, the prey.

Ironically, covering my terror that day with a polite rejection of the Oreo bait and my calm-but-steady motion away from him was my one and only Oscar-worthy performance. I might not have a statue to show for it, but I have my life.

Any Port in a Storm

The school bus deposited the Lawton trio at the end of the driveway. It was the late afternoon of January 10, 1954. We headed for the house trudging through snow drifts that were knee-deep to my regular-sized, eight-year-old legs. We kicked off our boots, opened the front door, and knew right away something was up. The quiet was too empty, the emptiness, too quiet. The note on the kitchen table told the tale. Billy and I hovered close to Polly as she read Mom's hurried handwriting aloud. It told us that Audrey (a high school senior from down the road) was coming to fix our supper and stay overnight with us because Dad had driven Mom to the Auburn hospital to have her baby. The note went on to say Dad would return home after the baby was born.

Our meal was guaranteed. Our orphan status would be short-lived. Reassured by the note, Polly, Billy, and I settled into homework, comic books, and *Nancy Drew and the Hollow Tree* in respective order.

Audrey arrived at suppertime. She had slogged the half-mile walk through drifts that were, by that time, knee-deep on a size regular seventeen-year old. She thawed out first, then fixed our dinner. After eating, all four of us acted stiff and unsettled because things just weren't feeling normal for anybody.

In the background the wind kept up a constant howl and shook our storm window frames. We watched two cars trying to get up our Mosher Road hill. Both backed down to try again. The intimidating drifts sent them back the way they came. The town snow plow had its own troubles with the hill. It backed down the hill twice, then powered its way up to the top, paused to take a breath and moved on to the flatter part of Mosher Road.

On calm nights we could see Tom and Isabell's house lights to the northeast. Not this night. Horizontal streaks of white snow sliced the cold, black air. That was all we could see. The phone rang, taking our focus off the dramas on the hill. When Audrey hung up the receiver, she first told us David Anthony, our new baby brother, had arrived. Then she told us to gather our pajamas and some other clothes. Our dad would be coming to pick us up and take us to our Auburn relatives to stay.

What? In the middle of the school year? We had more questions than Audrey had answers. My anxiety ramped up to match the weather outside. With our packed clothes on the floor in front of us, we sat stiffly on the couch wondering what was in store. The wind diminished just long enough to give us a glimpse of Marshall's house lights and a set of car lights on that stretch of Cork Street. It must be Dad, we agreed. He made the turn onto Mosher Road followed by a well-practiced run up the hill and into the driveway despite the pile the snowplow left there. He shoveled off the front steps and cleared a small path to the car, not his usual thorough job. Then he opened the front door and said, "Let's go."

Just as he spoke, a county sheriff's car with roof lights flashing pulled in behind Dad's car. The deputy's conversation with Dad at the door explained our situation. While Mom was busy having her baby, Dad was busy having appendicitis. The doctors wanted to operate immediately. Dad insisted they wait until after Mom delivered the baby. The doctors administered a shot of a painkiller which eased his pain through to the end of the delivery.

Then, he called home, spoke to Audrey and, unannounced, left the hospital to collect us. Mom got wind of this in her hospital room. Fearing for us all, she asked a nurse to call the sheriff.

Dad convinced both the deputy and us that he would be able to drive safely back to Auburn. He promised he would return to the hospital as soon as we were delivered to relatives. The deputy followed us halfway to Auburn then went his own way.

That sure was one wild ride into Auburn. Slipping, sliding, fishtailing through the drifts. I was delivered to Aunt Betty's and Uncle Tony's; Polly and Billy went to Aunt Rosie's and Uncle Dominick's. Dad went on to the hospital and into surgery.

Staying with my Fiduccia cousins for a week during summer vacation had always been a treat. This time, with my family scattered, both parents in the hospital, and my cousins in school all day, it didn't feel like a treat or a vacation. Aunt Betty did her best to keep me occupied, but the days were long and I grew restless being stuck indoors and not in school.

Kids and their germs were not allowed to enter hospitals as visitors. They were especially not welcome around newborn babies. While

Aunt Betty reassured me that my parents would be as good as new, those ten days of not seeing them seemed unending.

Finally, Uncle Tony gathered up Mom, Baby David, Polly, Billy, and me and drove us home. Dad stayed in the hospital.

We learned from overhearing Mom's telephone conversations with her sisters that she and most other adults thought Dad had made a reckless decision the night he drove in the storm to pick us up after taking painkillers. I thought Dad had been brave. My city uncles weren't experienced like Dad in driving the Scipio roads in winter, let alone winter storms. He took things into his own hands rather than letting others decide the fate of his family. He couldn't think of his own well-being until he had ensured ours.

"First things first," he liked to say.

When Dad recovered from surgery, Uncle Tony drove him home. There he stayed in bed for a good part of two weeks. At first, he was in a lot of pain. I delivered water and aspirin upstairs to Dad. Polly helped care for David. We kept David downstairs during the day and then upstairs with Mom and Dad at night. Mom, though tired and weak from giving birth, coped with a new baby, an ailing husband, and we three novice helpers.

We went back to school and everyone coped until a new normal took hold. However, a new normal doesn't always mean smooth sailing.

Baby David looked exactly like a Lawton except for his almond shaped eyes. We heard Mom tell other people that the doctors suspected David may have something wrong with him. But this suspicion was left vague and undecided for the meantime. I heard the word *mongoloid* used. It sounded scientific, harsh, and cold. Everything my baby brother was not. He smiled, he cooed, he laughed. He was a Lawton.

Unlike my dolls, David cried real tears. He cried when he needed to, not when it fit my storyline. At first, I wasn't sure I liked this big sister gig. But my responsibilities and Billy's were light compared to Polly's, who at fifteen, changed diapers, and could have stepped into much of Mom's role if needed.

Mom and Dad debated whether David met the milestone for smiling, or whether he had gas. But the debate waned as David became a frequent smiler, though some weeks off the mark. I showed him how to reach for his bright, noise-making, jungle gym objects, but he wasn't interested. When Mom said it was time for him to turn over, I tried to teach him, but gave up knowing he was happy to gurgle, wave his arms, and kick his legs. He smiled when I shook rattles, but he didn't reach out for them, though he grabbed onto my finger and wouldn't let go. David determined his own schedule of development and made progress on his terms, not ours.

At home and with relatives, I was at ease with David. But when he was six months old, we walked into a small diner for lunch. Dad carried David, the rest of us followed.

It's not unusual for seated patrons to watch new arrivals. I'd done it myself. But I noticed those who glanced up at Dad, then let their eyes rest on David with more curiosity than casual interest. Others looked up and away quickly as though they were uncomfortable. I felt the label of different slapped on David and on us. It made me sad for David and uneasy for me when my quiet nature liked nothing more than fitting in unnoticed.

When we'd finished eating, I saw the same long looks of curiosity on many of the patrons seated beside our path to the exit door. This time a sharp, orange anger pulsed through me. And I knew then, that protecting both David and my fragile ego was going to be a tough job.

All Hell Breaks Loose

Dad's stopping for a beer after work or a union meeting was not a problem for Mom or us. But that changed.

One afternoon we were cleaned up and ready to go to the Weedsport Fireman's Parade and Carnival. But Dad was late. As soon as his car pulled into the driveway, we flew out the front door. But Dad wobbled when he stepped out of the car, then picked me up and hoisted me over his head, laughing all the while. He didn't seem like the dad I was used to. Mom had some harsh words for him, but she must have made the decision he was okay to drive, as we all piled into the car along with an air of volatile tension. We were quiet for most of the ride. Dad's new demeanor scared me. I didn't feel safe with someone I didn't know, and I didn't know this new person. At the parade he continued to be more animated, louder, and sillier than the father I was used to. I kept my distance and my attention on the parade as much as I could. By the time the parade ended, and carnival started, he was more like himself.

After a few more similar incidents, life at home felt unsettled and on edge. Dad's work shift changed to 3:00 to 11:00 p.m. We were fast asleep by the time he arrived home. On several occasions I woke in the dark to arguing voices coming from downstairs. Mom probably stewed all day and now she spoke her mind thinking their conversations were off the record. While I couldn't hear all the words, I knew angry ultimatums were being tossed back and forth, suggestions that Dad go to Syracuse to live, words of separation and living apart. It never occurred to me that our family could disintegrate. How could I possibly choose one parent over the other? Who would I be, then? It felt as if I looked down, the earth would crack open between my feet. To save myself I would have to jump one way or the other–Mom's side or Dad's. So, I never looked down. Nor did I breathe a word of what I had overheard to anyone. I just let worry churn in my gut.

On May 29th, 1954, a Saturday, we woke as usual expecting Dad's car would be in the driveway. It wasn't. Mom was frantic. Before she collapsed into tears, she told us the police phoned to inform her Dad had been arrested and spent the night in jail. He had been drinking. Two U. S. Marines, home on leave, had been standing on the side of the road talking, when Dad's car hit them. Both were hospitalized with serious injuries.

I was scared for Dad. I was scared for the two Marines. I wished with all my might neither would die. As usual, my insides were in knots.

Later that morning, Mom left for Auburn to pay his bail. When she brought him home, a dense, dark storm of tension came in the door with them.

I could see Mom's blistering anger in the taut set of her lips. Dad's timid silence was pitiful. He didn't have to say a word, he reeked of shame. It was a relief when he went upstairs for a nap.

While he slept, Mom shifted into tirade mode. When Dad came downstairs Mom hit the ceiling. She may or may not have known I was in the living room as she pulled Dad in there from the kitchen.

She scolded Dad for shaming our family by being in jail, being reckless, and harming others. She walked him over to face the framed picture of the Blessed Virgin Mary which hung on the living room wall.

"Now I want you to promise the Blessed Mother that you will never take another drink. This has to stop."

Even the silent room gasped. I sure didn't understand. The Blessed Virgin Mary was Mom's belief, not Dad's. How would his vow to her (the BVM) mean anything? Either Mom's hysteria precluded rational thought, or she seized the sudden shift in power to add heathenism to an otherwise reasonable ultimatum.

To witness Mom's discipline of Polly or Billy felt awkward to me, even if I thought they deserved it. I empathized with their plight. But this was Dad. I saw and felt the searing pain of his diminished standing and his lost pride. I tried to make myself feel smaller. I willed myself to disappear into the sofa cushions, but I managed only the feeling small part.

"I promise," Dad said, in not much more than a whisper.

Mom got what she was after, Dad was free to go. He turned away from the BVM and toward the front door. His head was down and his eyes on the floor. He was smaller too. My shrunken father walked past me as I sat pressed into the sofa back. He lifted his head just enough to look at me. And his eyes delivered a silent message. His promise was not meant for the BVM. It was meant for me. Family is the first priority it whispered. And that gave me a splinter of hope.

Both Marines recovered. But one was still in a U.S. Naval hospital one year after the accident.

Witch Hazel

*M*eteorologists began tracking a tropical storm on October 5, 1954 as it rocked the islands of Curacao, Aruba, and Bonaire off the northern shore of Venezuela. On October 6th, it became a Category 1 hurricane and they named her Hazel. She picked up momentum spending October 7 and 8 as a Category 3. Hazel became an H4 and then turned northward. Having left a path of destruction and death across the Caribbean, Hazel made U.S. landfall October 14th on the Carolina coast with winds of 120 to 150 miles per hour. Her extraordinary forward speed of 55 mph meant she would travel inland farther than most hurricanes and keep most of her power intact.

On October 14th, our kitchen radio stayed on all day as reports came in about Hazel's force and probable direction. On Friday

Oct 15th, we stayed home from school; Dad did not report to his second-shift job. Instead, he battened down whatever hatches he found around the house and barn. Extra drinking water was drawn, kerosene lamps brought out. By lunch time we were as prepared as we could be for Hazel.

Just after lunch the wind picked up. It stirred up the tree limbs and stronger gusts rattled our windows. It grew darker outside as each hour passed. By midafternoon we lost electrical power. Dad drove to Tom Marshall's to help get Tom's cows into the barn. They started the chores early and Dad, Tom, and his hired help milked by hand.

Billy asked to bring his new beagle puppy, Duke, into the house overnight. Mom's no-animals-in-the-house policy stood despite our pleas and promises. Billy fed Duke, filled his water bowl, and tucked Duke and a blanket into his doghouse within the penned area under the horse chestnut tree.

In Mom's cedar chest, kept in velvet and satin luxury, sat two creamy white candles blessed several years ago by the bishop. Mom took them from their place of honor and stood them in candle holders. Our kerosene lanterns were lit against the darkness.

We ate cold sandwiches for supper while waiting for Dad to come home. Finally, around five thirty his car lights came into the driveway. He parked the car near the end of the driveway to keep it away from the black walnut tree limbs shielding its usual resting place. Billy and I went to the front door and watched Dad make his way in our direction. The wind blew straight at him from the south and whipped his pant legs and jacket sleeves out to the side. He held tight to his hat and leaned into the wind with all his might. He made slow progress toward the door, the wind forcing him backward a couple of times. As soon as he made it inside, we closed the door and locked it as though expecting a dangerous escapee from the Auburn prison to be on his tail. Dad ate supper, and we spent a quiet and anxious evening pacing around, looking out into the darkness and listening to the steady wind, the angry gusts, and the hard rain that pelted the house. Having no TV or radio was bad enough, then the telephone line went dead. Now it felt like we were truly on our own to face Hazel and whatever she had planned for us.

When Hazel grew louder and stronger, Mom lit one of the special candles. She fingered her rosary beads nonstop. Her lips moving silently with the prayers. I was already scared, but her zeal convinced me we were all going to die.

I don't know how much Mom and Dad slept that night, but we kids were ordered to bed at the usual times. I woke the next morning to the eerie, unsettled stillness after the storm. Light and brightness had returned, the wind had calmed, the rain had stopped. As I reached the bottom step, Billy came in the front door, Mom and Dad right behind him. Both Billy and Mom were crying, Dad's face was grim. Duke was dead. The huge branch that was holding my swing had broken off and crushed the doghouse and our puppy. It became another one of those painful events that we kids of the 1950s were supposed to just forget about. Except we couldn't, we didn't. And I'm willing to bet Mom didn't either.

Hazel was a serial killer. She killed 469 people in Haiti and 95 in the U.S. Fallen power wires electrocuted a mother and son in Auburn, New York. Hazel's murder spree swept right across the border into Ontario, Canada, where 81 people died, mostly in Toronto.

Newspapers duly reported the tragedies and to start the healing process included some humor as well. The day after the storm, the *Syracuse Herald Journal* reported that the movie marquee of the

Elmwood Theater had blown off in the brunt of the storm. The head-line read, "The name of the film? *Gone With the Wind*! And it was."

Hazel stole another chunk of my security. In its place, she left the fear of more storms to come. But I also have the memory of Hazel's darkest hour when a single candle's flame held all the hope there was. And all the hope we needed.

A Hard Row to Hoe

In the End Times when all is said and done and whether the earth ends by fire or ice, scientists predict that only viruses and cockroaches will survive. I know they haven't yet heard of the Lawton kitchen table, or it, too, would have made their short list.

It was made of Vermont rock maple. Aptly named, rock maple is a tough, densely grained wood. Heavy, strong, and stiff, it resists the everyday wear and tear that a family can throw at it. One source states rock maple may lack durability in exposed situations. I have proof, otherwise. Vermont, as its name implies, imparts a rural hardiness and a no-nonsense character. Considering the situations our kitchen table was exposed to, this extra protective layer of Vermont luster was key.

Eating lunch or dinner at our kitchen table coincided with Dad's daily practice of listening to WAUB radio's *News at Noon* or the

WMBO 6:00 p.m. local and national newscast. If Billy and I, sitting next to each other, slid into a fit of noisy bickering or giggles, Dad's clenched fist hit the tabletop. And we'd all jump. It happened with the speed and force of his former amateur prizefighter's jab. We didn't take it as a physical threat. But we knew Dad was agitated and we instantly changed our behavior if we could.

Mom said Dad's reaction to our background noise was due "to the Lawton-Sensitive-Hearing (LSH)" with which Dad was afflicted. She said it in a lighthearted way with a slight tinge of sarcasm. However, I understood her diagnosis to be a disease one should avoid catching. Now, however, I know LSH is a common trait of those who have the privilege of being an introvert. As an "Innie," I can hear an offending carrot-cruncher or ice-chewer from a distance of 150 yards. And if a husband talks while I'm in the midst of listening to something else (the Evening News) I have to shut one of them off or go berserk. *Berserk* means I go to my inner-Lawton-kitchen-table and pound the hell out of the insufferable noise.

The table also served as a work area for Mom when she cut and marked dress and curtain fabric. Only once did she slip with the tracing wheel leaving a line of seven dashes in the maple, looking like her tiny embroidery stitches.

The table was our homework desk, platform for building school projects, and once-a-year Dad spread out forms across it to file his income tax return. Yes, it had to be strong and flexible to serve us so well.

Under its main slab, the table had a hinged leaf stored underneath at both ends. We pulled one or both out and up to accommodate company or our new little brother and his high chair. Mom always complained that it needed to be wider to be more functional, but our dining space was in the kitchen and it fit just right as far as the rest of us were concerned.

Whether at its everyday-size or leafed out to full length, it was the gathering place that served as our communication hub; a story from Mom or Dad's youth, news of our relatives and neighbors, planning for the day's or week's events. It was also a place where a sister could spill the beans and get her bothersome brother in trouble and *vice versa*. Or we learned what our parents thought was humorous, or scandalous. It's where, through osmosis, we received our common education in who our parents were and who we were expected to be, by each other. We learned this among many grins, giggles, and Mom's tasty meat loaves. Mostly I remember it as a place where we sat in a circle around a square table and built who we were as a family.

Sometimes the table had to bear our worry or disappointments. On occasion, Dad would be laid off from his tool-and-die maker's job. We witnessed how our parents worried, how they made-do. Dad's "take things as they come" attitude combined with Mom's "fight-it and fix-it" demeanor was a powerful model. We learned not to expect too much for Christmas on those particular years. The table held meals of lesser nobility, but Mom was magic with pancakes and the vast supply of preserved food in the glass jars in the cellar. We never went hungry or felt the slightest bit deprived at mealtime.

We were called to the table one day in early 1955. It was not a mealtime, and the somber tone of voice and the unease with which Dad summoned us, and the fact it was Dad and not Mom were heavy hints this was serious. David, a year old now, napped in the next room. The rest of us took our usual spots at the table. We sat. Mom stood; a signal she was in charge and above the fray. Dad, who was keeping his promise not to drink, was there in a supporting role, but with a tinge of resignation. While their marital rift had narrowed it still seeped the pungent uncertainty of an open wound.

Mom started with the news Dr. Eisenberg and consulting doctors diagnosed David's condition as Down syndrome. It's a genetic abnormality, not an illness that can be cured she clarified. These doctors predicted he would have difficulty learning and would develop much slower than kids his own age. In the worst-case scenario, he wouldn't walk or talk and could be sickly. The doctors' advice was to place David in an institution because of the added strain my parents would incur, plus they had other "normal" children to think of.

"Our decision," Mom said, "after visiting two of these institutions, is to keep David with us as long as possible. It was heartbreaking to see all those babies and children alone, with no one paying attention to them. Placing him in an institution is a last resort. But we'll need your help too."

If Mom and Dad thought they'd get objections from the three of us, it didn't happen. I felt the blanket of sadness and uncertainty hover over us at the table. Could we do this? I imagined David living without us and felt the tears stinging my eyes. For the time being, I knew he'd be safe with us. I knew we loved him. Even more now.

Life's most significant and unforgettable moments, if viewed from above, are wrapped in a gauzy swirl of high energy that keeps it spinning through time. The rock maple, we at the table, the little one napping in the next room, the words, the breathing, the processing, the peering into the fuzzy future . . . each of these emitting and absorbing the vitality of the living moment.

Our rock maple moment pulsed first with our heartache, second with love, and third with a blind commitment. Then it whooshed away through time. And when another person or family needs such a fine, rich energy to sustain them, it shall find them, like it found us. And who knows what crisis, catastrophe, or gift of grace was responsible for its beginnings, nor how long it has been making the rounds.

Mom and David, Auburn, New York, 1954

Dad and David, Scipio, New York, 1954

David and Rusty

Weed 'em and Reap

Bernard Barry's death, a stormy January birth, a marriage in jeopardy, a serious auto accident, alcohol abuse, a hurricane, a pedophile, and a murky diagnosis. All of these trials, packed into a fifteen-month period, crushed my sense of security and slammed the brakes on our family's momentum. The Lawtons of Scipio had reached the brink of topple and crash. And there was no one in sight to wiggle the stick to set us spinning again. Well, there was. But we didn't know it just then.

Divorce among Hollywood couples was fodder for the gossip columnists in the 1950s. But it was far from common for mere mortals. In Scipio, among our relatives, and within the working class, divorce or separation was seen as a disgrace and a failure. There was no one I knew nor heard of then whose family was broken.

Though my family was mired in its troubles, we were still required to show up each day. To school, to work, to meals on the table. We had no Hollywood-type support staff to take over for us. Surprising and anticlimactic as it may be, carrying on with the stuff of every day might have been our cure-all.

David's daily well-being depended on all of us. His needs became family needs. We couldn't just ignore them, but, neither did his needs consume us. Sure, Mom and Dad shouldered the heaviest loads, but their soldiers in this cause were nine, twelve, and fifteen years old. And we marched to their beat.

There was no one day when I knew for sure we would stay a family. To my knowledge, I alone overheard the late-night ultimatums between Mom and Dad. There was no announcement of a truce. Over time, a quiet knowing crept into the atmosphere around me and nudged the uncertainty away. Maybe it was the same for them.

Mom and Dad joined the fledgling Cayuga County Association for Retarded Children (ARC). This group lobbied first for meaningful programs of education and employment for their children, and later on, for group home residences in the Auburn community. They held chicken barbeques to fundraise and advocated wherever they could on behalf of their special children. Mom basked in her advocate-activist role and did not shy away from chiding or petitioning politicians at the local, state, and federal levels to gain advantages for David and his peers. Joining with other families facing like-challenges gave us confidence and a sense of purpose and normalcy. Dad's quiet resourcefulness matched Mom's public activism.

On a hot summer day, in the car's trunk, alongside our inflated inner tubes, was a Dad-designed-and-built hinged, wooden frame. Suspended from this frame was a Mom-designed-and-sewn canvas baby-swing seat. At any and all lakes, David, the toddler, sat in his stable water swing, kicking and splashing in the shallows. Each of us taking a turn to stay near him. Family swims—no problem.

One summer day, when David was four years old, we were all busy indoors and out when Mom realized David was missing. In panic, we searched the house, the barn, and the roads in all four directions. After most of a panicked hour, we found him and his pet cat Rusty sitting under a hay wagon that was parked just off the edge of the yard.

David had become a wanderer. Therefore, a new Lawton Standard was decreed.

David must have one other Lawton with him at all times.

The Lawton tag team became a well-oiled machine keeping tabs on David. We never lost him again. Polly, Billy, and I still had our spats, but David leveled the playing field. In his eyes, we were equals; our rivalries had no meaning to him.

With time, David became the fourth of Mom and Dad's normal kids, the welfare of whom, the doctors had once been troubled. In their medical terms he was not normal, but he became a normal part of our normal day-to-day life. His delayed first steps stoked our fear of future disability. But when they happened, his first steps and all his firsts, were moments of relief and celebration. He needed supervision at all times. He needed reminders to use the bathroom. He needed us to guess the needs he was unaware of or didn't have the verbal skills to name.

As David aged into double digits, he continued to surprise us with unexpected skills. He had an infinite recall of details from his favorite TV shows, the *Dukes of Hazzard, Happy Days, Star Trek*. He perfected an imitation of Henry Winkler's *The Fonz,* with a thumbs-up "Aaay, aaay, aaay! His Tarzan yell, an octave higher than Tarzan's version, was unique and oh, so hilarious! He thought so too.

Dad lowered Billy's basketball hoop that hung on the front of the barn down to a lower but still challenging level. David shot hoops for hours. A plastic ball and bat developed his love of baseball and the New York Yankees. Tricycles, swings, he had everything we had as kids.

Most important, David had our magic side lawn in Scipio that oozed of athletic skill and stardom, real or imagined. On that patch of earth David believed he was a Syracuse Orangeman and Mickey Mantle, no less.

Billy nurtured David's sports acumen as he had nurtured mine. He encouraged David, not with horse chestnuts, but with patient coaching.

Gentleness was the main ingredient in everything we did with him and for David. He taught us well.

David loved music. He sang along to all of his 45-rpm records and cassette tapes in his wide collection. David Cassidy and David Lawton were one and the same person, he claimed. In his attempts to convince us of this, he flashed a hopeful, conspiratorial smile. We, of course, caved in.

He gave us private performances employing his nieces and nephews as backup singers. He executed his rhythmic and unique dance moves among his peers at various functions. Trophies and awards piled up as he swam, dove, and bowled with the Special Olympics. He developed some basic mechanical skills in a sheltered workshop for which he earned wages. His life was full and he was happy.

David's inner life, though, was a mystery to me, one I wanted to understand. He spoke in short sentences and phrases, never able to verbalize his thoughts or feelings. I watched his facial expressions and body language for clues. Since he was a Lawton, a shoulder shrug was familiar. But since he was David, some, like repetitiveness, was syndrome-based.

David's normal states of being were joyful, calm, and trusting. He rarely seemed frustrated and lacked any expression of anger. After infancy, David cried tears only three times in his life that any of us know about. First, in his teens, the one time he was sick with a high fever. Next when Dad died, and then, again, upon Mom's death.

David on his Scipio swing

Children and adults with Down syndrome have such an enormous capacity for joy that it spills over and infuses anyone nearby. David was no exception. He made us laugh, he made us cry, he tested our patience, and he made us love as we had never loved before.

David's was the hand that wiggled the stick and restored our family momentum. He was the glue that held us together. He was our gift.

In the Lawton garden, we were weeds growing in disarray, until David lined us up and taught us how to flower.

Kathy, Billy, Polly, Niagara
Falls, Canada, 1955

Seeds of Change

Around the age ten or eleven, I shuffled the well-scuffed toes of my Buster Browns to the edge of the big puddle. The child in me begged to wade in and splash to my heart's content. But a new voice inside me begged to differ.

"You know," it said, "there might be more mud in that puddle than you've bargained for. Sure you're ready?"

While my bruised and bandaged Guardian Angel sat outside on my right shoulder whispering, this new entity inhabited my inside. Its voice sounded familiar, but since it came from the far end of a shadowy tunnel, I couldn't identify it.

All around me things were changing. Billy still needed me to hold the catcher's mitt as a target while he practiced pitching. But, that was about it. The rest of the time he helped Tom Marshall part-time or he and his buddies rode their bikes all over Scipio, swimming at the quarry, camping out in the woods overnight. When his friends were around, Billy acted like he hardly knew me; like I was in the way.

My playmates and classmates were on the same edge as me. Barbie loosened her grip on dolls and make-believe once she had her own horse. Competition in athletics and scholastics grabbed at me and my classmates. We were once a solid herd of little classmates with a "we're all in this together" attitude. Then egos and personalities emerged to form like-minded splinter groups.

Like most children, I let go of childhood in sporadic dribs and drabs. Then the pace picked up. The barn lost its magical charm. My dolls were abandoned in the haymow's classroom after Ed Sullivan brought Elvis into my living room one Sunday evening.

Dad got quite a kick out of Elvis. Mom, with David on her lap, uttered a few tsk, tsks at his dance moves followed by her girlish giggle. Polly rolled her musically sophisticated eyes as if to say, "gauche, tacky, hillbilly." But she watched just the same. Billy, well, I couldn't tell, except he moved his head to the beat. I had no words for Elvis's appeal. But that strange, new, inside voice came to the rescue. It squealed.

My last pair of Buster Browns gave way to a cool new pair of black-and-white saddle shoes. I wore them to school, I wore them to sock hops, and then I wore them to the edge of the puddle and toward my future.

The voice I couldn't quite identify turned out to sound just like me. It was shaky, unsure, shy. But it, too, had learned to abide by the Lawton Standards.

I waded in.

⁂

Smack Dab
in the Middle

An introvert with a heavy dose of empathy has little time for self-actualization when pigeon-holed to be a sounding board. My listener-in-the-middle role began as a first grader. A bashful boy classmate, (let's call him John) sat at the desk in front of me. On a Monday morning he turned and whispered to me that he liked the girl behind me. Would I mind, he added, telling her of his declaration. At lunchtime she declared to me that she liked him, too, and would I tell him? The two never spoke to one another. Their entire affair was conducted through me. In the classroom, in the cafeteria, and on the playground, I passed messages. Then, on Friday, they broke up.

My short career as matchmaker transitioned to a lifelong career as peacemaker. At first it was unruffling Mom and Dad's respective feathers by listening, staying neutral, and staying quiet. As a kid, this role was a balancing act.

> *You had to be the center of the seesaw so the pain flowed **through** you, not **into** you. It was very hard. But she could do it!*
> —Terry Pratchett, *I Shall Wear Midnight (Discworld, #38)*

In my midthirties, I felt like Charlie Brown's friend Lucy had hung a sign on the front of my office desk: **Psychiatrist: Five cents.**

A trickling parade of needy coworkers sought my ear. One, worried about the impending birth of his first child asked, "But, what if I don't like the kid?"

Being a fixer of problems, a cheerleader, and a peacemaker for others was easier than to fix myself. I wanted to be a better me, a better parent, friend, and employee. I forced myself to take steps (baby steps) toward the dark side—extroversion.

A library of self-help books accumulated. They promised to turn me into a confident, off-the-cuff speaker instead of stuttering and stumbling and reading from a script. I was urged to be assertive instead of aggressive. As if! I learned that *I'm OK-You're OK*, except I wasn't and neither were you.

Then one day, tired of the effort it took, I stood on the proverbial rooftop and shouted,

"You know what, World? This is as good as I get. Deal with it."

Of course, no one but me heard it, because, well, I shouted it quietly.

At long last, a flood of validation poured into my e-reader when in 2012 I downloaded Susan Cain's book, *Quiet: The Power of Introverts in a World That Can't Stop Talking*. Wow, Susan Cain gets me! Now I get me! The "Innies" have been outed and we are more than just okay, we are valuable. A lifetime of self-doubt washed away in that flood.

The next fix? My fear of being prey, courtesy of the Scipio pedophile.

My husband, John, and I picked up Historic Route 66 in Illinois. Our destination was its destination, California's Santa Monica Pier. We hit the brakes when we spotted a sprawling roadside lot in Arizona displaying hundreds of vintage autos. We each walked our separate path through the maze of shiny pimped out '57 Chevys, Cadillac Eldorados, and muscle cars with Shaker scoops. After a half-hour's meandering, as I lifted my head to get my bearings, I came face-to-face with a blue panel truck identical to the one driven by the Scipio pedophile. It startled me. I froze. I expected the familiar panic to rise. It did not.

A few months earlier, from their deep hiding place, I dredged up the facts and feelings of that incident. I transformed them into inanimate words made of dried ink on flat, unemotional paper. In this nonthreatening, one-dimensional form, two truths became clear.

First, I was not to blame. Fear, shame, and guilt belonged to his story, not mine. Those malignant emotions lost their power over me.

Second, (forgive my triteness) I found the silver lining. An innocent little country girl used the power of her quiet nature, to thwart bold evil.

✿ I observed the small details: his truck parked on the wrong side of the road, again!

✿ I recognized the anomalies: both doors open, his nonchalant posture leaning against the truck.

✿ I acted on instinct and intuition: refusing the Oreo cookies to keep my distance. I offered a believable excuse, "No, thanks, they'll spoil my supper."

✿ I mirrored his nonchalant posture by keeping a consistent pace pushing my scooter. If I'd panicked and speeded up, he may have done the same to prevent his prey from escaping. Perhaps he was overconfident and had no back up to the Oreo cookie plan.

In case I've overstated the effect of my quiet superpowers, I'll admit that my battered and beleaguered Guardian Angel may have been on back-up duty that day. If so, her name that day was Grace. 'Twas she who led me home.

Uprooted

On a warm September day in 1981, Dad and I sat in lawn chairs, side-by-side, looking out over the hillside we'd planted with a thousand pine seedlings almost twenty years prior. We were deep into our usual pattern of conversation.

Silence. Unbroken silence. Strong enough to hold each of us in our own thoughts while somehow sensing the other's. Then, from Dad, a soft, "You know, I'd just as soon die here."

Dad's natural thrift with words meant they carried the weight of the world if they had to. In this case, they had to. Those eight words conveyed Dad's bone-deep sorrow at having to leave, explained his sense of duty as the reason, acknowledged my pain, and asked for my forgiveness.

Another moment of silence passed, then my response, "I know."

Mom made the decision. Dad surrendered. Our Scipio property was sold to a neighboring farmer and an apartment in Auburn awaited them. As usual, they preplanned every detail including how to dispose of their yard and barn sale leftovers. Wily parents, indeed, who targeted me, their sentimental pack rat. Whatever hadn't sold and whatever I could haul away was mine. How they must have grinned with smug pleasure when they hatched that plan.

I packed my car to the roof for the trip home to Rochester, New York. Among the treasures were a half-dozen of Dad's unsold tools, the lone surviving alphabet block from David's Fisher-Price pull-along wagon, Mom's potato masher circa 1940, and other treasures too many to name and all priceless except for the offending sale tags. Clearing enough front seat room for me, I was almost ready. But one last thing to do.

I walked to the end of the driveway and turned down the road to visit our little stone house. I needed to say goodbye to this symbol of childhood. Dad renamed it the *Leprechaun House* to suit his Irish heritage once his small grandchildren began to visit. When either they or Dad's Sensitive Lawton Hearing needed soothing, he would whisper,

"Shhhhh, if you are quiet, we can hear the Leprechauns."

A magical hush followed, expectations heightened, and many claimed to have heard the wee people. Peace and quiet ensued and all were happier.

On that last day, fifty yards short of the little house something stopped me at the crest of the hill. My feet felt rooted in that spot and I closed my eyes. The warm autumn breeze stirred up an earthy fragrance of fresh-cut grass, spicy cedar, road dust, and a hint of musty golden maple leaves drying aloft in the sun. Breathing deeply, I tried to inhale this place and this moment into my mind, my body, and my soul forever. This place and I melded into one. The sense of belonging overwhelmed me.

Then, I felt them crowding around me; the presence of many. They were faintly visible in my closed-eyed vision, but fully present. With me. Some adults, some children. Some Native Americans, some farming families from days gone by. They seem to stand with me in reverence, of what, I didn't know then. Somehow, they sensed the depth of my sadness and loss, and somehow, they eased my fear of letting go.

A half-dozen years went by with the memory of that moment remaining vivid. But I couldn't always keep the tears at bay. More loss, more goodbyes as my own children left the nest. Then, I met John, and my second marriage took me to live in Ontario, Canada. One Sunday afternoon we visited Petroglyphs Provincial Park. Its carvings in the smooth, sloping rock, made by ancient First Nations people, represented figures of their spirituality. Shamans, animals, perhaps, the Great Spirit. My rock-loving and storytelling nature transcended the centuries to bond with the ancient carvers. We spoke the same language; quiet and enduring.

We followed the path into the Learning Place Visitor Centre, its displays and self-guided tour deepened the story of the site and its people. Halfway through the Centre, my eyes were drawn upward to an opening to the next display room. Across its archway, in stylish text, was written a quote attributed to Rina Swentzell, Pueblo.

What we are told as children is that people, when they walk on the land, leave their breath wherever they go. So, whenever we walk, that particular spot on the earth never forgets us. When we go back to these places, we know that the people who lived there are in some way still there, and that we can partake of their breath and of their spirit.

At Loose Ends

Nowadays, wooden barns are an endangered species. Structures made of metal frames and synthetic roofs dot today's farming landscape. They are used to shelter livestock, store farm equipment, and preserve baled hay and straw. I've not, yet, seen one with a nurturing space for a child's imagination. Our Scipio barn, built around 1865, was vintage and well on its way to becoming antique, when we acquired it in 1946.

Its unknown builder never wavered from the design principle of form-follows-function. Dad and our animals found it functioned just fine, a star performer. Mom, however, could not find in its stoic form, a single hint of pleasing aesthetic. It was plain, it was patched, it sagged a little; okay, more than a little.

My eyes did not judge the exterior. They saw only its magical cavernous space on the inside, where anything was possible, even me.

As long as a wooden barn houses large animals, the structure's wood absorbs moisture from the animals' perspiration, breath, and droppings. Emptied of the animals, the barn wood dries out, shrinks and cracks. Weather-worn and time-worn, the barn stiffens, shifts, and weakens.

Our weary barn watched in resigned silence as the animals paraded away, sealing its fate. The large animals first, followed by the small animals and birds. Saddest of all was when the reckless kids packed up their laughter and lives and moved to faraway pastures, and other barns of possibility.

The early 1960s saw Polly became a competent surgical nurse who, according to Polly, saved many a surgeon's ass during her career. She married, moved to Pennsylvania, and raised two lovely accomplished daughters. She is *Grammie* to four beloved grandsons who excelled in all the sports she'd loved as a spectator, especially baseball.

As adults, Polly and I, both married with children, discovered we had much in common. Our six-year age difference no longer a barrier, we mutated into two loving, sharing, caring sisters. Who would have guessed? We'd become close and of one mind. We could finish each other's sentences or fill in the gaps whenever one of our aging brains seized.

But, never, ever did we discount the value of the demilitarized zone between us: the northern half of Pennsylvania, all of New York State, and later on, the Canadian border. Polly and Billy continued to refer to me as "The Brat" throughout the years until November 2016, when sadly, Polly passed away.

Bill(y) joined the U.S. Navy after high school, served in the Viet Nam war, married, and had a son and a daughter and several outstanding and accomplished grandchildren. Bill continues to terrorize me, though now it's by flipping a barbed joke or an embarrassing truth my way. However, I never forget, he still carries a gun.

I married soon after graduating from high school, moved to the Rochester, New York, area and formed my own family. A son, first, then three daughters. During their childhood years, we spent many weekends visiting Grandma, Grandpa, and Uncle Dave in Scipio. Today, I have seven awesome grandchildren and one shining great-grand child; plus I'm the "wicked" stepmother to John's children and grandchildren in Canada.

I now know why Mom's penchant for labeling irritated me. Limitation. I'm thankful she never acquired a DYMO® label maker until I'd left home. Mom's need to identify then fix a problem was a caring one. She wanted the best for me. Her idea of the best. But my need was to branch out in all directions and try on what felt right. To Mom, this was treason. Her version of "damn kid" was her frequent and exasperated, "That's right, missy, just go your own way!"

No single label can tell the truthful story of any one person, ever. I'm proud to march under the flag of Introvert, but to my own beat.

Curiosity never lost her grip on me. My yearn-to-learn is unstoppable. I prefer to be self-taught. I choose my own path to learning. A course in statistics seemed irrelevant when what I needed to know in-depth was the accounting cycle. The many college-level courses I took had to have direct application. Am I autodidactic? Yes, but there are resulting holes in my knowledge base. Enter Google, libraries, on-line courses.

Label me a polymath if you must; a person who has expertise in many areas. My career life has spanned small business management, communications, accounting, payroll, advertising, marketing, and human resources management. I'm a shapeshifter. But label me wife, mother, grandmother, sister, daughter, friend, and I won't bristle. Living, liking, and loving has been my finest career.

Aging dissolved the adhesive that lets those pesky labels fall away. Faced with a gentle cascade of failing body parts and the prospect of another decade or two, I lightened up on myself. Now, I peacefully accept me and my life, warts and all. My criminally insane math and algebra skills summed the pros and cons. And came to this conclusion:

I've lived a damn good life. This last part? Unlimited playtime. Unlimited ice cream.

As for my siblings, David remained with Mom and Dad until his midthirties, then thrived in an Auburn group home with three long-time housemates and their Seneca-Cayuga ARC staff. Each of my trips back home centered on a visit with David for drives, walks, pizza, and ice cream cones.

Bill was David's legal guardian, monitoring his care and his activities. I was back-up guardian while Polly advised on David's health care. For David, we were still a team and did our best to ensure the Lawton Standards stood firm.

A decade after our property's new owners had taken possession, I took David on a car ride past our old Scipio property. I slowed halfway up "our" hill to glimpse the Leprechaun House, and as I reached the top of the hill, I saw, since my last drive-by, the barn had given up and fallen flat. Its noble and eternal rest was well earned. I was saddened. I didn't stop. Like Miss Laurel, I took my time driving the rest of Mosher Road, blinking away tears.

When David was born, Down syndrome adults rarely lived past their forties. David was sixty-four years of age when he passed away in August of 2018. He and his signature smile were well-known rays of sunshine throughout Auburn and the far reaches of his community.

Sunday Go to Meetin'

*T*he number of non-Lawtons enchanted by the Leprechaun House is known only to the wee folk. Burton Minde invited then neighboring Mosher Road farmer Ronnie Walters, a former schoolmate of mine, to walk to church with him one Sunday morning during the late 1970s. Burton, a generation older than Ronnie, gave no further explanation. Ronnie took a leap of faith. The two of them walked eastward down Mosher Road until Burton stopped. Their place of worship? The Leprechaun House. Something tells me Burton might have known Miss Laurel.

Ronnie's grown sons, now brawny farmers themselves, still visit the little stone house that once captured their own childhood hearts. They clear away the brush that grows up around it. Serious plans to dig up this little treasure and move it to one of our homes were hatched by my children and their cousins. Polly, Bill, and I were torn. We understood their desire to keep it in the family. But we cautioned them that moving it may destroy it. Besides, I had hoped that any children from Miss Laurel's family might one day want to find it. Or Miss Laurel herself, might come back for a visit. Maybe she did.

After all, Miss Laurel knew, like I did, that Scipio's soil holds memories of ancient times, of the beginning of time, of hunting parties of the Cayuga tribe, of old-time farmers and schoolmarms. And Scipio's rock and stone hold and protect the very heart of the Finger Lakes.

The little stone house remains where a loving father built it, keeping safe the dreams of children. In lives that sometimes go adrift, it's an anchor, that will bring them back to who they were, who they hoped to be, and who they may be yet.

Walking the Edges, Reprise

*W*hile my legal surname is no longer Lawton, I've stayed true to my birthright. My home in Canada sits atop a hill, on ten acres of land once part of the old Tennyson family farm. I am surrounded, not by eleven, but by the hundreds of lakes in Haliburton County.

Walking the edges of this h'lawton-like property, I follow a fallen wire fence line partly buried in soil. It rises to where, in several trees, the wire's grown an inch deep into the bark. Woodland has reclaimed this once rocky pastureland. The pillars of this community, my staunch guardians, number in the hundreds.

Here, where destiny dropped me, Mother Nature's glacial irony is not wasted. Fronting our house is a north-south running hill that looks suspiciously like a drumlin. Not only that, but looking out to the east, someone opened the oven door too soon and the land just dropped to the valley below. This is me, still living on the edge.

Here, I write, my laptop perched on the Lawton kitchen table. Despite the dings and dents of time, its Vermont rock maple luster imitates the dinged, dented, but durable marriage of Mary and Bill Lawton of Scipio.

Elsewhere in our home are more Scipio leftovers, too many to mention, but all still priceless.

In a quiet corner of our home, artfully mounted on a rustic cedar-plank wall, are Dad's self-healing hammer, vintage carpenters' square, wood planer, and hand-operated drill. His still-stylish level, aged to full retirement, holds its place of honor overseeing the rest.

Its strong presence whispers, "Keep your balance, be the center, be yourself, damn kid!"

Acknowledgments

I am forever grateful to all who have contributed to *Stone House Stories.*

My editor, Sheryl Loucks, for prying loose from my introverted pen, the twenty-thousand additional words that filled in the blanks and rounded out the story. Your inner child and mine live close to the surface and have a blast on their playdates.

Photo editor extraordinaire, Tammy Rae, for the generosity of her time, skills, and enthusiasm in covering up the evidence of my decades of careless photo handling. You're a brave cosmetic surgeon willing to take a stab at anything!

Brenda Peddigrew and members of the Algonquin Highlands Writing Circle who first heard many of these stories in their infancy and provided generous dollops of resonance; especially my Monday Morning Muse, Pat Brown.

Early readers, Jennifer Purc and Gina Stanley, who provided valuable insight and the encouragement to carry on.

The Haliburton Writers and Editors Network, the Reading Writing Connection, the Arts Council of Haliburton and the Haliburton County Library System, and Friends of the Library, for sponsoring excellent events, nurturing my desire to become an author.

My husband, John, for his patience and understanding when dinners were delayed or forgotten; and for cheering me on to the finish line. Thanks, Hubs!

My brother, Bill, for a decade of reading each iteration of *Stone House Stories* from its first, thin, five-page version through to its present form; love ya, Baaaaar-t!

My kids, Robert, Barbara, Susan, and Lory and my awesome grandkids, for spurring me on by asking for "more, please, more."

My relatives-from-the-distant-past, especially the poets, journalists, and storytellers, for donating the strands of DNA that make me who I am for better or worse. You can stop prodding now.

My entire present-day family for lighting each day with love and laughter. You put the "peep" in the peepers. You make the cloudy days bearable. You are the hopeful stars in the dark night sky.

And to Bodhi Ray's generation and my family-of-the unknowable future, especially the poets, journalists, and storytellers. I challenge you to keep our story going. Write it as a thriller, film it as a fantasy, create a mystery. Skip the crime and horror genres. Whatever you make of it, always and forever make it a love story.

I hope you enjoyed this book. Would you do me a favor?

Your opinion is invaluable. Would you take a few moments to share your assessment of my book on Amazon, Goodreads, or any other book review website you prefer? Your opinion will help the book marketplace become more transparent and useful to all.

Thank you very much!

Visit me at my website *www.kathylawtonpurc.com* and email me at *kathy@kathylawtonpurc.com.*

For More Information:

Finger Lakes Tourism Alliance

309 Lake Street, Penn Yan, New York 14527

800-548-4386; 315-536-7488

https://www.fingerlakes.org

Life in the Finger Lakes (magazine)

171 Reed Street, P.O. Box 1080, Geneva, New York 14456

800-344-0559; 315-789-0458

https://www.lifeinthefingerlakes.com

Quiet: The Power of Introverts in a World That Can't Stop Talking (book) by Susan Cain

The Quiet Revolution (Susan Cain website) https://www.quietrev.com

Arc of Seneca Cayuga

1083 Waterloo Geneva Rd, Waterloo, New York 13165-1202.

Phone: (315) 856-8152. Email: aventura@arcsencay.org.

https://thearc.org/chapter/arc-of-seneca-cayuga

9 781777 105808